The Problem of God
A Short Introduction

Peter A. Angeles
Santa Barbara City College

PROMETHEUS BOOKS
Buffalo, New York

Published 1980, 1986, by Prometheus Books
700 East Amherst Street, Buffalo, New York 14215

ISBN 0-87975-216-5

Library of Congress Catalog Card Number: 73-85469

Printed in the United States of America

To my wife Elizabeth
and to our
children
Beth, Jane, Adam
all in fun and love

Preface

The Problem of God: A Short Introduction is an introductory book planned for use in Introduction to Philosophy courses during the three to five week section which deals with problems in the Philosophy of Religion. The book may be used in conjunction with other books such as those suggested in the bibliography, in introductory courses in the Philosophy of Religion, and in Comparative Religions. It can be used to satisfy both a general education requirement for students as well as provide a foundation for those who plan to take a more advanced course in Philosophy.

The material is philosophically (as opposed to theologically or religiously) oriented, stressing the problem of God as a logical and philosophical problem. The perspective is critically analytic in the Naturalistic-Humanistic tradition. The basic approach is an issues or problems approach, but this is set in a historical context with quotations from Greek philosophy, the Church Fathers, the Medieval period, and from modern philosophers. The aim is to enable students to *see* what is being said and has been said about God and thereby fit this into a better framework in the light of present knowledge and society. It is hoped that students will develop an awareness and appreciation of the philosophical problems in the concept of God, that they will acquire the ability to engage in intelligent evaluation and exchange of ideas, and that they will display these qualities in their everyday thought.

This volume is by no means exhaustive of all the themes in the Philosophy of Religion. The most fundamental ones about God's existence are covered thoroughly. The book is a starting-point for more intensive work in the subject. It lays down the basic groundwork for an easy transition to other topics and to more sophisticated thought-patterns. The writing has been kept as concise and elementary as possible with short sections on a variety of topics. The titled sections and numerical ordering of each chapter make it convenient to organize the material according to the interests of the teacher and the students. The numbered sections facilitate easy cross-references.

I wish to express my deep appreciation to my sister, Mrs. Virginia Fanos, for typing and retyping the manuscript—for her perseverance, patience, and kindness. Special thanks go to my wife who carefully proofread the manuscript and who made many suggestions about the content and format as the work progressed. Thanks to Al DeSimone who assisted in the drudgery of reading the first draft, and to Adam Sebestyen, UCSB Librarian, for his helpful references and comments. I am also grateful to the many students and faculty these past years at the University of Western Ontario and at Santa Barbara City College who have encouraged me. My gratitude also to editors Roger Ratliff and Linda Gambaiani who assisted in the preparation of the manuscript—it was indeed a pleasant experience working with them. Thanks to Dr. Paul Kurtz and Jerry Koren who facilitated this edition. It has been a pleasure working with Prometheus Books.

Contents

VI God as the Necessary Being: The Sufficient Reason for Existence 81

VII God as the Cosmic Mind 99

I

God as Completely Perfect

1.1 Introduction. The ontological argument for God's existence begins with a definition of God and then proceeds to show that God's existence in reality is made necessary by that definition. "Ontology" means "the study of Being." It comes from the two Greek words, ὄντος meaning Being, and λόγος meaning to study the underlying reasons why a thing (in this case 'Being') is the way it is. The word ontology is often used interchangeably with the word metaphysics, which refers to the philosophic attempt to understand in a comprehensive way the nature of reality as an interrelated whole.

The approach in the ontological argument has been called a priori (as opposed to a posteriori). The truth of the premises in the argument does not rely upon experiencing the external world in a certain way. The procedure is from the *essence* of God to His *existence.* One begins with an idea of God and from this idea the existence of that God in reality independent of the mind is deduced.

The a posteriori approach proceeds from an examination of things in reality such as motion, causes, effects, order, design, purpose, to a definition or idea of God who exists with certain kinds of characteristics. The truth of the premises in the argument depends upon what we observe in our experience of the world. This procedure is from an analysis of what exists in the world to a description of God's Being—from existence to God's essence.

1

The roots of the ontological argument for God's existence can be traced back to Plato (427 B.C.–347 B.C.) and to Augustine (354–430). In its various forms it has been propounded by numerous thinkers: St. Anselm (1033–1109) presented the first systematic formulation of the argument; St. Bonaventure (1221–1274); René Descartes (1596–1650); Benedict Spinoza (1632–1677); Gottfried Wilhelm Leibniz (1646–1716); Hegel (1770–1831); and in modern times Karl Barth (1886–1968); Paul Tillich (1886–1965); Charles Hartshorne (1897–); Norman Malcolm (1911–).

The ontological argument has always had its critics: Gaunilo, dates unknown but a contemporary of Anselm's who critically replied to Anselm's arguments; Thomas Aquinas (1225–1274); Caterus, a Catholic priest who was a contemporary of Descartes; P. Gassendi, another contemporary of Descartes; David Hume (1711–1776); Immanuel Kant (1724–1804); Arthur Schopenhauer (1788–1860); Bertrand Russell (1872–1970); Gilbert Ryle (1900–).

1.2 Anselm's Formulation of the Argument. Saint Anselm was the son of a nobleman, born at Aosta in Piedmont. He became a Benedictine monk in Normandy in the Abbey of Bec. Over the years he was appointed through the ranks until he became Abbot, and in 1093 he replaced his former teacher, Lanfranc, as Archbishop of Canterbury.

Anselm's two most important works were his *Monologion* and his *Proslogion*. The *Proslogion* may be thought of as the culmination of several goals: (1) He wanted a simple argument whereby the necessity of God's existence could be proven abstractly without reference to concrete existing facts or things. The simpler and purer the abstraction, the more uncontroversial and convincing would it be; (2) He wanted an argument which would begin with an indubitable truth about God's being which would serve as a premise in an argument which would flow with certainty into the conclusion that "God exists"; (3) He wanted an argument that was so beyond any possible doubt to anyone at all who could understand the meaning of the terms employed, that it would be utterly compelling, requiring a transformation from disbelief to belief; (4) He wanted to attain a logical or mathematical precision and certainty about God's existence. The statement "God does not exist" must be shown to be as inconceivable as a "square-circle" or a "round-square." Holding the position that there is no God would then indeed be as foolish as believing in contradictions such as "square-circles" and "round-squares"; and (5) He wanted a description of God and an argument for God which would emphasize his religious feeling that God must not only be a Being of Magnificent Greatness but must not be limited by anything greater than Himself. God cannot be surpassed in supremacy. He must be that Being upon which all things owe their being. All things owe their creation to Him. All things owe to God all that they are, have been, and will be, without exception. All things depend upon Him but He depends on nothing else outside His own existence. God cannot merely happen to exist. Things happen because of God, but God does not "happen" for any reason. His essence is existence. God must exist and everything else must depend on His necessary existence. God's nonexistence is unthinkable. The existence of finite things is unthinkable without this God. These things Anselm found in his definition of God as *that than which nothing greater can be conceived*. From the *Proslogion*:

CHAPTER II. THAT GOD TRULY IS

O Lord, you who give understanding to faith, so far as you know it to be beneficial, give me to understand that you are just as we believe, and that you are what we believe.

We certainly believe that you are something than which nothing greater can be conceived.

But is there any such nature, since "the fool has said in his heart: God is not"?

However, when this very same fool hears what I say, when he hears of "something than which nothing greater can be conceived," he certainly understands what he hears.

What he understands stands in relation to his understanding (*esse in intellectu*), even if he does not understand that it exists. For it is one thing for a thing to stand in relation to our understanding; it is another thing for us to understand that it really exists. For instance, when a painter imagines what he is about to paint, he has it in relation to his understanding. However, he does not yet understand that it exists, because he has not yet made it. After he paints it, then he both has it in relation to his understanding and understands that it exists. Therefore, even the fool is convinced that "something than which nothing greater can be conceived" at least stands in relation to his understanding, because when he hears of it he understands it, and whatever he understands stands in relation to his understanding.

And certainly that than which a greater cannot be conceived cannot stand only in relation to the understanding. For if it stands at least in relation to the understanding, it can be conceived to be also in reality, and this is something greater. Therefore, if "that than which a greater cannot be conceived" only stood in relation to the understanding, then "that than which a greater cannot be conceived" would be something than which a greater can be conceived. But this is certainly impossible.

Therefore, something than which a greater cannot be conceived undoubtedly both stands in relation to the understanding and exists in reality.

Chapter III. That It Is Impossible To Conceive That God Is Not

This so truly is that it is impossible to think of it as not existing.

It can be conceived to be something such that we cannot conceive of it as not existing.

This is greater than something which we can conceive of as not existing.

Therefore, if that than which a greater cannot be conceived could be conceived not to be, we would have an impossible contradiction: That than which a greater cannot be conceived would not be that than which a greater cannot be conceived.

Therefore, something than which a greater cannot be conceived so truly is that it is impossible even to conceive of it as not existing.

This is you, O Lord our God. You so truly are that you cannot be thought not to be. And rightly so.

For if some mind could conceive of something better than you, the creature would rise above its Creator and would judge its Creator, which would be completely absurd.

Also, whatever else there is, except for you alone, can be conceived not to be.

Therefore, you alone, of all things exist in the truest and greatest way (*verissime et maxime esse*), for nothing else so truly exists and therefore everything else has less being.

Why, then, did the fool say in his heart: "God is not," since it is so obvious to the rational mind that you exist supremely above all things? Why because he is stupid and foolish.[1]

1.3   Gaunilo's Criticism. Anselm's argument was criticized by a monk of Marmoutier near Tours named Gaunilo. Gaunilo's argument was

---

1. John Hick and Arthur C. McGill, eds., *The Many-faced Argument, Recent Studies on the Ontological Argument for the Existence of God* (New York: Macmillan, 1967), pp. 4–7. Copyright 1967 by The Macmillan Company and used with permission.
   Other easily accessible sources for this passage with slight variations in translations: Alvin Plantinga, ed., *The Ontological Argument from St. Anselm to Contemporary Philosophers* (Garden City, N.Y.: Anchor Books, Doubleday, 1965), pp. 3–5, and John Hick, ed., *The Existence of God* (New York: Macmillan, 1964), pp. 25–27.

critical of the way in which Anselm proceeded from an idea (a thought, an essence, a definition) to a reality existing separately from the idea. Nothing can be defined into existence. If that were not true, then could not anything at all equally be defined into existence?

According to Gaunilo, one cannot deduce the existence of God from one's idea of Him. Suppose one has an idea of a completely perfect island with perfect sand, perfect waves, perfect food, perfect mermaids, perfect weather, perfect clouds, and perfect palm trees. The idea of such a completely perfect island is in the mind and can be said to be understood. But because it exists in the mind as completely perfect does this entail that it must exist also in reality? For Gaunilo, it would be absurd to argue that the completely perfect island must exist not only in the understanding but also in reality, because it is more of an excellence to be in reality as well as in the understanding. For Gaunilo it is mistaken to assume that unless this completely perfect island exists in reality then another island which *does* exist in reality would be more excellent than it—thereby what we have initially defined as the completely perfect island is *not* the completely perfect island (because the one that has real existence is!)

Anselm's reply to Gaunilo is that the argument about the completely perfect island—or for that matter any comparable argument dealing with any specific, particular concept, or thing in the Universe—is correct. Anselm clearly understands the difference between something existing only in the mind and something existing as well in reality. But Anselm insists that he is not talking about any specific, particular thing. Anselm is talking about God—a Being "that than which nothing greater can be conceived." According to Anselm, Gaunilo's argument applies to all things except to God. It is true of every particular existing thing that it can be conceived not to exist. That is, whatever exists can be thought of as not existing. This is true of everything except God. God, for Anselm, is the only Being which cannot be thought of as not existing. God is a Necessary Existence—a Necessary Being.

1.4   The Hume-Kant Criticism: Existence Is Not a Predicate. Is it more of an excellence to exist than not to exist? Assuming, as Anselm did, that to exist is a primary good, and assuming God is a "Supreme Good," then the answer would have to be in the affirmative.

But is it more of an excellence to exist in reality than to exist only in the mind? Anselm partly rests his argument on the assumption that just as when we say "God is Good," "God is Love," "God is Merciful," "God is Just," we are adding a property to God, so when we say "God Exists" we are also adding a property.

Anselm's assumption is that existence is an attribute or property. Since God is "that than which nothing greater can be conceived," He then cannot lack existence—if He did, He would then be lacking something which would limit his greatness and He then would not be "that than which nothing greater can be conceived."

What is this quality or attribute which God "lacks" if He does not exist in reality? Is real existence something such that when it is not present in a thing this then deprives that thing of some excellence, or quality, which it cannot have unless it did exist in reality? What kind of property is existence which when *not* present, would in effect produce a lesser being—and when *present* would produce a greater being than one that did not possess it? Can a concept be just as perfect, or excellent, and not exist in reality? Is it possible that it can be more perfect as an idea in the mind and becomes imperfect once it is exemplified in reality?

The Hume-Kant criticism of the ontological argument is based on the notion that existence is not a predicate. David Hume originally presented the idea in his *Treatise*:

> The idea of existence, then, is the very same with the idea of what we conceive to be existent. To reflect on anything simply, and to reflect on it as existent, are nothing different from each other. That idea, when conjoined with the idea of any object, makes no addition to it. Whatever we conceive, we conceive to be existent. Any idea we please to form is the idea of a being; and the idea of a being is any idea we please to form.[2]

Kant, who named the argument the "ontological" argument, developed this idea in his first of three *Critiques*:

> [4.] *Being* is evidently not a real predicate, or a concept of something that can be added to the concept of a thing. It is merely the admission of a thing, and of certain determinations in it. Logically, it is merely the copula of a judgment. The proposition, *God is almighty*, contains two concepts, each having its object, namely, God and almightiness. The small word *is*, is not an additional predicate, but only serves to put the predicate *in relation* to the subject. If, then, I take the subject (God) with all its predicates (including that of almightiness), and say, *God is*, or there is a God, I do not put a new predicate to the concept of God, but I only put the subject by itself, with all its predicates, in relation to my concept, as its

---

2. From the book *A Treatise of Human Nature* by David Hume. Intro. by A. D. Lindsay. Everyman's Library Edition. Published by E. P. Dutton & Co., Inc. and used with their permission.

object. Both must contain exactly the same kind of thing, and nothing can have been added to the concept, which expresses possibility only, by my thinking its object as simply given and saying, it is. And thus the real does not contain more than the possible. A hundred real dollars do not contain a penny more than a hundred possible dollars. . . .

By whatever and by however many predicates I may think a thing (even in completely determining it), nothing is really added to it, if I add that the thing exists. Otherwise, it would not be the same that exists, but something more than was contained in the concept, and I could not say that the exact object of my concept existed.[3]

Existence is not an attribute of a thing as red, pungent, small, or hard are attributes of a thing. The word "exists" does not describe anything as do these other predicates. Existence is not a predicate to be added to a thing whereby our concept of it is enlarged or altered. We are not descriptively changing our concept of a thing when we say that there actually exists in the real world a thing of which it is a concept. We are not saying that the concept of a thing is greater, or more perfect, when we say that it also exists in reality, or when we say that we can find an example of it in reality. When we do find an example for our concept and say that "it exists," we then do nothing more than make clear that our concept does indeed apply to something beyond itself. But whether or not our concept does apply to something outside itself can never be ascertained merely by examining the concept itself.

To say that X has properties y, z, o, p, q and then to say that that X also has existence is not to add anything to that X—we still have the X with the properties y, z, o, p, q. To say that X exists is to say something *about* that X with its properties y, z, o, p, q. We are saying that we believe it can be found to exist in reality beyond its mere conception. This is not adding a characteristic, or a property, or an attribute.

For Kant there is no difference between these two statements:

(a) I have an idea of a mermaid with properties y, z, o, p, q, and

(b) this idea I have of a mermaid with properties y, z, o, p, q also exists in reality.

---

3. Theodore Meyer Greene, ed., *Kant Selections* (New York: Charles Scribner's Sons, 1929), pp. 248–49. Used by permission of the publisher.

Supposing actual, real existence did add a property to my concept of that mermaid. What would it be? A different color? More scales? Longer hair? If asserting that my idea of a mermaid really existed *did* alter the properties contained in my idea, then the existing mermaid could not have been the same as that of which I had an idea—it would be another idea.

For Kant, a hundred imaginary dollars have all the predicates of a hundred real dollars. If existence did add something to the concept of a thing, then the existing thing would be something more, or different, than what the concept was. We then would not be in a position to say that the object of our concept exists. If a hundred real dollars and a hundred imaginary dollars did not have the same predicates then we would not be able to compare our concept of the thing with the real existing thing in order to discover whether or not our concept was correct or could be found to exist in reality.

Certainly the actual *existence* of a concept is a matter of considerable importance. A thousand real dollars in one's pocket does make a difference to one's buying power—something which a thousand imaginary dollars do not. Finding that the concept has an actual referent is also a matter of considerable importance to one's better formulation of the concept (ignoring for the moment also the importance to one's *formation* of a concept). Finding our concept of a mermaid behind a rock at the beach would beyond any doubt make a tremendous difference in altering our concept of a mermaid. We possibly now see the particular peculiarities of actual mermaids which our concept did not previously take into consideration, such as the size and shape of the scales, the weight, the color of her hair, the shape of certain parts. Saying that our concept exists does not affect the concept—but seeing it in existence may. Our seeing our concept of the most Supremely Perfect Being would change our concept of Him. Saying that He exists does nothing to the concept of Him, except perhaps implying the hope that an example of Him can be found actually existing, which is the very problem at hand: Can such an exemplification of God be found?

Thus to say that our concept "exists" is to say that the concept has some real external object to which it refers, that there is at least one example of our concept, that our concept has a denotation. Our concept of God as "that than which nothing greater can be conceived" is not enlarged, or changed, or added to by also saying that this concept of God exists. Since existence is not a property, it then is not a property that any Perfect Being might lack or possess. Since existence is not a property, then even if "that than which nothing greater can be conceived" does not exist in reality, it would still be by definition "that than which nothing greater can be conceived" (but of course only existing in our minds).

1.5   The Form of the Argument. Anselm follows a *reductio ad absurdum* argument form. Assume that God exists only in the understanding but not also in external reality. If this were so however then God would not be that which He has been defined as being, namely, "that Being than which nothing greater can be conceived." Why? Because it would be possible to conceive of a Being who would be the same in every other way, except that it existed as well in reality, thereby making such a Being greater than the identical being which existed only in the understanding. This is admitting an absurdity—or a contradiction of the initial definition of God. It is admitting that God is a Being than which a greater can be conceived. Thus what we assumed at the beginning of this paragraph (that God exists only in the understanding) must be false (since it leads to a contradiction). The only consistent and true conclusion must be that God exists both in reality and in the understanding (if He is to be "that than which nothing greater can be conceived").

The necessary existence of God is apparent when it is seen that a Being that cannot be conceived of as not existing is greater than a Being that can be conceived of as not existing. If you could conceive of God as not existing, then God would not be as great as a Being that cannot be conceived as not existing. There is thus a clear contradiction in holding on the one hand that God is a Being "that than which nothing greater can be conceived" and on the other hand that that God does not exist.

But this contradiction which Anselm points out would really exist only for the person who *did* hold to the belief that God was, indeed, "that than which nothing greater can be conceived." The success of the *reductio ad absurdum* form of the argument depends upon an acceptance of the original premise as being sound. (We can know that some contradictory concepts such as "square-circles" do *not* apply to anything in reality, but we cannot proceed from a logically possible concept to the conclusion that it does exist in reality merely on the basis that its nonacceptance would involve a contradiction. How do we proceed to an acceptance of that definition of God rather than another one? What happens if that meaning of the word "God" is not accepted?)

Anselm meets this sort of comment with this argument: If someone understands God as such a Being "that than which nothing greater can be conceived" and *does not* understand *that God also to exist in reality,* then he does not understand the meaning of God as that Being "that than which nothing greater can be conceived." When someone understands God as a Being "that than which nothing greater can be conceived" and also understands that that God exists, only then does he have a true understanding of the meaning of God as "that than which nothing greater can be conceived."

But this involves circular reasoning: understanding the concept of God is understanding that He exists and if we do not admit His existence we have not understood the concept of God. The concept of God is contingent upon His existence. It is similar to arguing: If you really want to stop smoking you would. (If you really understood the concept of God, you would see that God exists.) You haven't stopped smoking because you really don't want to. (You don't accept God's existence, because you really haven't grasped its concept.)

According to Anselm, anyone who has a true understanding of the meaning of the word "God" can see by merely analyzing this meaning of the word "God" that it is self-contradictory to hold simultaneously that "God does not exist" (or that God exists only in the understanding). But this self-contradiction is created by the definition itself. If existence is part of the very meaning of the term "God," then to say that "God exists" is a tautology and true by definition like the statements: "Bachelors are unmarried." "Apples are apples." (A is A.) "Red apples are red." (A is AB.) It is contradictory to the definition of "bachelor" to assert that it is not the case that bachelors are unmarried. It is contradictory to assert that it is not the case that "apples are apples." It is a self-contradiction to claim that it is *not* the case that "red apples are red." The truth of these statements is undeniable. Their falsity is inconceivable. Their truth is guaranteed by the definitional and logical form of the statements themselves. Statements such as these (often called tautologies or analytic statements) repeat in their predicate what is already assumed in the subject with whose meaning we have already begun.

Thus if the essence of God is existence, then by definition it would be contradictory to say that God does not exist. But *is* God's essence, existence? Could there be something else as well whose essence is also existence, such as matter, energy, the Universe? If existence is made the defining characteristic of God, then the conclusion "God exists" must be necessarily true since it follows from the definition in our premises. *If* God is "that than which nothing greater can be conceived," and *if* existence is necessary for Him to be "that than which nothing greater can be conceived," then God certainly exists—necessarily and without any logical doubt. But the task still at hand is to go from that definition of God in the *if* clause to that clause's existence in reality—to show that the definition has an exemplification.

Similarly, it is logically necessary that a triangle has three angles. If it did not it would not be called a "triangle" in our usage of that term. This "necessity" is essential to the definition of the word "triangle." The necessity lies in the analyticity of the proposition itself and *not* in its necessarily existing in reality, or in any actually existing triangle that we can examine. There is no "empirical" necessity that a triangle with three sides exists. But *if* a triangle exists, then it *must* necessarily, by definition, have three angles. You cannot go from the "necessary" characteristic of a statement (logical necessity) to the "necessity" that it exists in empirical reality. This is another way of saying that the *denotation* of a concept can never be contained in the concept itself. Not even the concept of God as "that than which nothing greater can be conceived" can, from its mere assertion, have actual existence assured for it.

If the definition of God ("that than which nothing greater can be conceived") is synonymous with Complete Perfection then the ontological argument may be presented in this fashion:

(1) God is *The* Completely Perfect Being.

(2) Existence is necessary for anything to be Completely Perfect. Therefore,

(3) God exists (as The Completely Perfect Being).

If the argument can be presented in this way, and if the argument is seen as logically valid and sound, then with just a few slight changes another diametrically opposed argument can be constructed which also would be logically valid and sound.

(1) God is *The* Completely Imperfect Being.

(2) Existence is necessary for anything to be Completely Imperfect. Therefore

(3) God exists (as the Completely *Imperfect* Being).

We have now shown God to be "that than which nothing worse can be conceived." Who is to say that one cannot assume existence for Complete Imperfection? Of course that Completely Imperfect Being would not be named God in our tradition. By whatever name we have an argument for a Completely Perfect Being and a Completely Imperfect Being. (In another sense of "Perfect" they are both Perfect: One is Perfectly Perfect and the other Perfectly Imperfect. Does this then mean at least two Gods?)

1.6 What Does God as "Necessary Existence" Mean? There are three metaphysical dimensions implicit in Anselm's concept of God as "Necessary Existence."

(1) Phrases such as "Thou canst not be conceived not to be"; "God is a Being whose non-existence is inconceivable"; "God is a Being who has the characteristic of never-being-able-to-be-conceived-as-not-existing"—may be construed to mean Eternality. God is eternal.

There are existences such as rocks, men, tables, chairs, and clouds that have beginnings and ends in time. All of these particular existences have at some time or another not been what they presently are. None have been forever what they are. They all can be thought of as being nonexistent at some time. They are thus "nonnecessary" beings.

In contrast, God is the existence that always was and always will be without Beginning and without End. God does not come into being or pass out of existence. God can never be conceived as coming into existence or passing out of existence. God cannot ever be thought of as not being in existence at some time or another.

To the extent in which "Necessary Existence" is identical in meaning to Eternality to that extent Anselm is presenting a concept accepted since the time of the Pre-Socratics, namely, that it is an indisputable metaphysical truth that something must exist which is eternal, without Beginning or End. This is an inevitable conclusion of thought which cannot be denied. If it is denied one then must assume such logical impossibilities as: The Universe (Existence) came from absolute Nothing, or the Universe can be annihilated into absolute Nothing.

The problem of course is that that Something which exists eternally does not have to be a Being, or Anselm's God. It could just be an eternally existing Matter. But perhaps there is nothing that remains the same in an Eternal Time—not even Matter. Perhaps it is the case that some kind of Universe is in existence in some form or other at any moment in Eternity but nothing that remains the selfsame infinitely into the past and infinitely into the future.

What are the arguments to convince us that there is an Eternal Being, and that Eternal Being is a God? If such an Eternal Being called God can be shown to exist, why couldn't He be co-eternal with the Universe (Matter, Existence). If co-eternality is a possible alternative, there are then two things which possess this characteristic of "Necessary Existence"—God and the Universe. This is something which Anselm himself might not tolerate.

(2) There is a Platonic implication in Anselm's concept of "Necessary Existence." Only particular beings have parts. Only beings composed of parts can be thought of as being nonexistent. God (like the Platonic conception of the soul) has no parts. Therefore God cannot be thought to be nonexistent. God is in existence all the time and cannot be thought ever not to have existence. And since God is in existence all of the time then He has no parts.

Beyond the circularity involved in this argument there are two assumptions that have to be accepted: (a) That God is a Being that has no parts. (Assuming that this can be made intelligible.) (b) That because beings composed of parts can be thought of as nonexistent this then is good reason to argue that beings without parts cannot be thought of as nonexistent—that is, that beings without parts can only be thought of as being eternal. But perhaps things with no parts also can be thought of as nonexistent. Perhaps things with no parts also can become nonexistent at some time or other and are therefore not eternal.

(3) "Necessary Existence" also can be seen to mean for Anselm: All finite beings depend for their existence upon a Being (God) that does not depend for Its existence upon anything else other than Its own Self-Sufficing, Eternal Existence. It is inconceivable that such an Eternal Being which supports, sustains, organizes, and maintains finite beings in order to be what they are rather than becoming something else does not exist. (This approach when followed through leaves the realm of arguing "ontologically" or in an a priori manner and argues a posteriori.)

We shall be discussing this meaning of "Necessary Existence" in subsequent chapters, but we might keep two basic questions in mind: (a) How can it be shown that there is such a Being which exists apart from contingent events which sustains the particular order we have in the Universe to occur as it does which when taken away leaves chaos? Is there such a Being that is the source and underlying ground of the beginnings and ends, changes and processes, of all finite particular things in the Universe? (b) Is it necessary to assume such a Being for an adequate explanation of events in Nature? What does such a "Sustainer" explain? What sustains the Sustainer? Are there impelling intellectual reasons to refer finite contingent events to a "Necessary Being" upon which they depend for their very existence?

1.7 What Does "That Than Which Nothing Greater Can Be Conceived" Mean? (1) It means that *God is a Completely Perfect Being.* But what does "Completely Perfect Being" itself mean? An understanding of a sort can be had by using the concept of a "completely perfect" ax. It can be said to be completely perfect with respect to the function of cutting up wood or chopping down a tree. When used for the purpose of scratching my back or for paddling a canoe it is less than completely perfect. There can even be a kind of understanding about a completely perfect triangle (definitionally), a completely perfect drawing, a completely perfect love. It is more difficult but still somewhat possible to talk about *The* Completely Perfect ax; *The* Completely Perfect Triangle; *The* Completely Perfect Drawing.

But what would it mean to talk about *A Being,* or *The Being,* which is Completely Perfect? The other concepts in the above paragraph are *things* gauged to be "perfect" *in some respect or other* and "perfect" *relative* to other functions and things. If God is The Completely Perfect Being, then *what kind of Being is He* and in *what respects is He Completely Perfect,* and *relative to what is He Completely Perfect?* For Anselm He is a Pure Being in Himself without parts, Completely Perfect with respect to such attributes as Love, Power, Justice, Mercy, Goodness, Kindness, Truth, Beauty, Eternal Existence, and He is assuredly Completely Perfect relative to His creatures and Nature. God truly exists more completely and fully than all other beings. All other beings have lesser reality and being than God. They derive their reality, perfection, and being from this Completely Perfect Being.

When stress is put on Anselm's concept of God in this way it turns into a kind of argument used years later by Aquinas known as the *Fourth Way*—from the gradation to be found in things. But must there exist a Completely Perfect Good (or Love, or Mercy, or Truth, or Beauty) from which any particular good derives its being and in comparison to which any particular example of a good is known and whose worth is judged?

Apart from the problem of what Love, Goodness, Kindness, or Mercy to a Perfect Degree could mean is the problem that such attributes may be merely names for personal human responses to situations that are charged with emotion and that they may not have any existence in an objective reality.

(2) What does "greater" mean in the phrase "that than which nothing greater can be conceived"? We have seen that following Anselm's usage it generally means more perfect, more excellent, more superior. But does existence make a thing more perfect? Is existence a perfection? How is a perfect definition of a circle made more perfect by its existence? Perhaps its very existence detracts from its perfection. We never find in existence a perfect exemplification of our "perfect" definition of a circle. (Might it be as in some Eastern religions that instead of existence being necessary for perfection, "nonexistence" in reality is necessary for perfection?)

We do often say that the "real" thing is better than the "imagined" thing. But sometimes we say that for something *not* to exist in reality is better than for it to exist in reality (for example, dying of leprosy). At other times we may even admit that a thing's existence in fantasy is better than its existence in reality—for example, depending on the neurotic conflicts involved, nonexisting sexual fantasies may be more pleasurable than their reality.

It is not whether something exists in reality which always makes a thing more perfect, more excellent, or more superior. It is the *quality* of our subjective response to it, and/or the quality that we see it to have which makes it perfect (or imperfect).

This argument may not be thought to be so compelling with reference to *power*. A *power* that does *not* exist *in reality* is surely less excellent, and less perfect, than power that does exist in reality. But this really means that an imaginary power is not as efficacious upon reality as real power. This is true, but that is not the point at issue. Superman is more powerful than any conceivable existing mortal even though he never has actually existed. In what way would he be still more powerful if he had real existence?

(3) The phrase "that than which nothing greater can be conceived" implies a maximization principle. "Greater" in the context of the definition is not a completed predicate. To have meaning it must be limited, "maximized," or completed at some point. But can all properties be maximized? Can there be a maximum for such things as power, knowledge, love, goodness, perfection, justice? Can some of these even be thought of in terms of a maximum-minimum quantitative type analysis? "Greater" suggests such potentially quantitative things as "more," "larger," "bigger," "more magnitude." If they *cannot* be "maximized," and if they nevertheless are included as attributes of God, then this is inconsistent with the concept of God as a Being "that than which nothing greater can be conceived" since some greater attribute would be conceivable. But if they can be maximized we have not the assurance that there may not still be a *greater* in that respect that can be conceived. How do we know that we have arrived at the maximum?

If it is argued that "love," "knowledge," "goodness," "perfection" are of a special Divine kind unlike the human kind, which can be maximized to a Highest Degree, then it is hard to understand what meanings could intelligibly be given to this special kind of Divine "Love," "Knowledge," "Goodness," and "Perfection" which are different from any ordinary sense of these terms, and far different from any sense applied to man.

Must not the "Power," "Love," "Knowledge," "Truth" of God somehow be like ours that we experience (but "greater")? If they are not in any way like ours, then how can such divine attributes be made intelligible? If God's divine attributes are inconceivable in themselves, but nevertheless "maximizable" in a way never to be known by man, then how can these divine attributes be made meaningful?

(4) The phrase "that than which nothing greater can be conceived" contains no specific reference to any of God's attributes (yet it can be made to incorporate *any and all* the traditional attributes anyone would

want to give Him). The definition provides a structure into which any and all attributes of the good kind can be fitted. But it offers no way of finding out what those attributes are, which *are* to be fitted into the structure. This is left to depend either on other nonontological types of arguments, or divine revelation, or what we feel God ought to be like if He were to be a God (or if *we* were to be God).

(5) According to Anselm in order for God to be "that than which nothing greater can be conceived" (The Completely Perfect Being), He must possess all attributes that a proper God should have which consistently go together. But there are attributes of God's Perfection that do not seem consistent. Anselm himself points out these kinds of difficulties (*Proslogion*, chapters IX–XI). For example, Perfect Mercy and Perfect Justice do not cohere: A Perfectly Merciful God would forgive all our sins; a Perfectly Just God would punish all our evils.

Phrases which claim to describe God, such as "God is the Supreme Good," "God is Completely Perfect," "God is Love," hold true by virtue of the way in which we want to talk about God. They are held as being true descriptions because of our feeling that a proper object of worship must have these characteristics. No one would want his God to be less than these things. It is essential that God must have these characteristics if He is to be labelled by the word "God." If one denied that God did possess those characteristics one then would not be talking about God (as far as our tradition is concerned). Thus it seems linguistically and conventionally necessary that God have these attributes—but that there is a Being that has these attributes is the very point at issue. The word "God" may not be a label for anything. We may be merely involved in implying that the word "God" must have these characteristics (by our definition) if it is to have that meaning which we want such a word to have.

II

God as the First Mover:
The Unmoved Mover

2.1 Introduction. The classical presentation of the "cosmological" arguments for God's existence are found in St. Thomas' *Summa Theologica.* As presented there together they have been called the Five Ways. They are called "cosmological" because they attempt to show the existence of God from premises which contain in them facts about the sensed world or about the cosmos. We shall classify all the five arguments as cosmological. Some commentators do not regard the fourth one as cosmological; some regard only the first two as cosmological.

Thomas Aquinas was born of a noble family in 1225 near Naples. In 1244 he became a Dominican friar. He studied and taught in such places as Paris, Cologne, the Papal Court, and Naples. Albert the Great was one of his teachers from whom he learned a great deal and for whom he had much respect. Aquinas was one of the most profound thinkers in the history of thought and one of the most prolific writers of all time.

Here are the Five Ways simply presented in the *Summa Theologica*:

> *We proceed thus to the Third Article:—*
>
> *Objection 1.* It seems that God does not exist; because if one of two contraries be infinite, the other would be altogether destroyed. But the name God means that He is infinite goodness. If, therefore, God existed, there would be no evil discoverable; but there is evil in the world. Therefore God does not exist.

Obj. 2. Further, it is superfluous to suppose that what can be accounted for by a few principles has been produced by man. But it seems that everything we see in the world can be accounted for by other principles, supposing God did not exist. For all natural things can be reduced to one principle, which is nature; and all voluntary things can be reduced to one principle, which is human reason, or will. Therefore there is no need to suppose God's existence.

On the contrary, It is said in the person of God: *I am Who am* (*Exod.* 3:14).

I answer that, The existence of God can be proved in five ways.

The first and more manifest way is the argument from motion. It is certain, and evident to our senses, that in the world some things are in motion. Now whatever is moved is moved by another, for nothing can be moved except it is in potentiality to that towards which it is moved; whereas a thing moves inasmuch as it is in act. For motion is nothing else than the reduction of something from potentiality to actuality. But nothing can be reduced from potentiality to actuality, except by something in a state of actuality. Thus that which is actually hot, as fire, makes wood, which is potentially hot, to be actually hot, and thereby moves and changes it. Now it is not possible that the same thing should be at once in actuality and potentiality in the same respect, but only in different respects. For what is actually hot cannot simultaneously be potentially hot; but it is simultaneously potentially cold. It is therefore impossible that in the same respect, and in the same way a thing should be both mover and moved, i.e., that it should move itself. Therefore, whatever is moved must be moved by another. If that by which it is moved be itself moved, then this also must needs be moved by another, and that by another again. But this cannot go on to infinity, because then there would be no first mover, and, consequently, no other mover, seeing that subsequent movers move only inasmuch as they are moved by the first mover; as the staff moves only because it is moved by the hand. Therefore it is necessary to arrive at a first mover, moved by no other; and this everyone understands to be God.

The second way is from the nature of efficient cause. In the world of sensible things we find there is an order of efficient causes. There is no case known (neither is it, indeed, possible) in which a thing is found to be the efficient cause of itself; for so it would be prior to itself, which is impossible. Now in efficient causes it is not possible to go on to infinity, because in all efficient causes following in order, the first is the cause of the intermediate cause, and the intermediate is the cause of the ultimate cause, whether the intermediate cause be several, or one only. Now to take away the cause is to take away the effect. Therefore, if there be no first cause among efficient causes, there will be no ultimate, nor any intermediate, cause. But if in efficient causes it is possible to go on to infinity, there will be no first efficient cause, neither will there be an ultimate effect, nor any intermediate efficient causes; all of which is plainly false. Therefore it is necessary to admit a first efficient cause, to which everyone gives the name of God.

The third way is taken from possibility and necessity, and runs thus. We find in nature things that are possible to be and not to be, since they are found to be generated, and to be corrupted and consequently, it is possible for them to be and not to be. But it is impossible for these always to exist, for that which can not-be at some time is not. Therefore, if everything can not-be, then at one time there was nothing in existence. Now if this were true, even now there would be nothing in existence, because that which does not exist begins to exist only through something already existing. Therefore, if at one time nothing was in existence, it would have been impossible for anything to have begun to exist; and thus even now nothing would be in existence—which is absurd. Therefore, not all beings are merely possible, but there must exist something the existence of which is necessary. But every necessary thing either has its necessity caused by another, or not. Now it is impossible to go on to infinity in necessary things which have their necessity caused by another, as has been already proved in regard to efficient causes. Therefore we cannot but admit the existence of some being having of itself its own necessity, and not receiving it from another, but rather causing in others their necessity. This all men speak of as God.

The fourth way is to be taken from the gradation to be found in things. Among beings there are some more and some less good, true, noble, and the like. But *more* and *less* are predicated of different things according as they resemble in their different ways something which is the maximum, as a thing is said to be hotter according as it more nearly resembles that which is hottest; so that there is something which is truest, something best, something noblest, and, consequently, something which is most being, for those things that are greatest in truth are greatest in being, as it is written in *Metaph. ii.* Now the maximum in any genus is the cause of all in that genus, as fire, which is the maximum of heat, is the cause of all hot things, as is said in the same book. Therefore there must also be something which is to all beings the cause of their being, goodness, and every other perfection; and this we call God.

The fifth way is taken from the governance of the world. We see that things which lack knowledge, such as natural bodies, act for an end, and this is evident from their acting always, or nearly always, in the same way, so as to obtain the best result. Hence it is plain that they achieve their end, not fortuitously, but designedly. Now whatever lacks knowledge cannot move towards an end, unless it be directed by some being endowed with knowledge and intelligence; as the arrow is directed by the archer. Therefore some intelligent being exists by whom all natural things are directed to their end; and this being we call God.

Reply Obj. 1. As Augustine says: *Since God is the highest good, He would not allow any evil to exist in His works, unless His omnipotence and goodness were such as to bring good even out of evil.* This is part of the infinite goodness of God, that He should allow evil to exist, and out of it produce good.

Reply Obj. 2. Since nature works for a determinate end under the direction of a higher agent, whatever is done by nature must be traced back to God as to its first cause. So likewise whatever is done voluntarily must be traced back to some higher cause other than human reason and will, since these can change and fail; for all things that are changeable and capable of defect must be traced back to an immovable and self-necessary first principle, as has been shown.[1]

All of the Five Ways are elaborations of concepts taken directly from Aristotle and indirectly from Plato. Following the footsteps of his teacher Albert the Great, Aquinas presented a defense of Christianity in Aristotelian terms. More and more translations into Latin of Aristotle's works were appearing at the time through Arab influences. Aquinas did not read the texts in the original Greek. No basic conflict was seen to exist between Aristotle's philosophy and Christianity. Aristotle was called *The Philosopher* by Aquinas' age and was rarely disputed but modified and used to substantiate the Christian faith in as rational a way as possible.

2.2   The First Way: The Argument From Motion.

(1) Motion exists—things change.

(2) Things are moved by other things and do not move themselves.

1. Anton C. Pegis, ed., *Introduction to St. Thomas Aquinas* (New York: Random House, 1967), *Summa Theologica*, Q. 2, Art. 3, pp. 24–27. Used by permission of the publisher.
   This passage is found in many anthologies. Two good and inexpensive paperback editions either of which would be useful with this textbook are: John Hick, ed., *The Existence of God* (New York: Macmillan, 1964), pp. 82–85, and Donald R. Burrill, ed., *The Cosmological Arguments, A Spectrum of Opinion* (Garden City, N.Y.: Anchor Books, Doubleday, 1967), pp. 52–56.

(3) And these other things do not move themselves but are themselves moved by previous things.

(4) These motions cannot go on ad infinitum into the past. There cannot be an infinite regress of motions, and movers, because then nothing would have begun to move at all.

(5) There must therefore be a First Mover, or an Unmoved Mover, who initially moved all things but is Himself unmoved by anything. That we call God.

The above is a way of presenting the argument to show the horizontal, or temporal, feature of the argument. God is the initial member in a time-series who starts the whole process. Here is a way of presenting the argument to show a "vertical" or ultimate ground feature of the argument:

(a) Motion exists—things change. There is motion which is not only a change of space or of place. It is the motion of moving from a state of potentiality to a state of actuality. The wood is potentially hot. Fire makes it actually hot. A child is potentially a man. (What is it that makes the child actually a man?)

(b) There is a Prime Mover who supports and maintains the states of development (motions, changes) of Being itself. God is the highest or last level to which we can appeal to explain all other change and all these changes are subordinate to the Source for this World-Order. Thus the Prime Mover is the Underlying Ground or Necessary Being that makes a thing what it is rather than its becoming something else.

Both the first two Ways (Motion and Cause) have this temporal or horizontal characteristic which stresses an initial source of the series. We shall discuss this characteristic in detail with reference to the Second Way and an Infinite Regress. All of the Five Ways have the other "vertical" feature of Ultimate Ground, Necessary Being, Supreme Governor, or Creator of Values. We shall discuss this vertical feature in more detail in subsequent chapters dealing with the other Ways.

The following are some of the basic assumptions in the First Way: It is not possible that moving things can derive their motion from a series that stretches back infinitely. The Universe of itself cannot produce an initial motion to get itself moving. The Universe was at one time in a static state (or the Universe was nonexistent and God created *ex nihilo*—out of nothing.) The Universe could not have changed of itself from this static nonmoving state to a moving state. The Universe does not contain its own eternal source of motion but receives it from a transnatural source outside itself. Things cannot move of themselves. There is no such thing as self-motion or self-movement of matter, or the Universe.

Most of these assumptions about the Universe need not be made. There are alternative views. For example, with reference to the denial of self-motion, the Greek and Roman Atomists (Leukippos, Democritus, Epicurus, Lucretius) held that motion was an intrinsic property of eternally existing atoms and atoms did not need forces outside themselves to become activated. There never was a time when the Universe did not, or could not, exhibit the property of self-movement.

Plato, on the other hand, in criticizing the materialistic philosophies of his time assumed that the soul is a "motion which can move itself" *(Phaedrus)*. Souls are simple self-activating principles and *sources* of motion in inanimate things *(The Laws)*. The movement even of heavenly bodies is caused by these self-moving souls. Plato worked from the presupposition that living things could not come from nonliving things, mind cannot come from something that does not contain mind in it, motion cannot come from things that are static but only from eternally moving things such as souls. Matter for Plato did not have its own power of motion. It could not move itself. This is close to Thales' hylozoism, or sometimes called hylomorphism: "All things are full of Gods"—that is, energy, forces, self-movement. Plato himself in *The Laws* quotes this passage from Thales (585 B.C.) who is regarded as the first philosopher of the Western world.

Can the notion of an Unmoved Mover be made intelligible? How can something give motion to something else without itself moving? What moved the Unmoved Mover to move the Universe? What previous motion was the source of that first movement? Does this then lead us into an infinite series of divine motions prior to that first movement of the Universe? Is the notion of a "static" Universe—a Universe composed of inert matter prior to a giant impetus given by God at a first moment in time—contradictory? (That is, by definition is it the case that matter to be matter cannot be inert but must be in continual activity and in motion?) If God existed eternally up to that first motion, what was He doing up to that time and what was He like? Why didn't He create earlier than He did? Is God co-eternal with the Universe? Or did He create the Universe (and its motion) "out of nothing"—or is this in any way possible? Perhaps the Universe has no Unmoved Mover, or First Mover, but has always been in motion eternally?

In general, Aquinas' position is pervaded with the Platonic-Aristotelian tradition regarding the divine and the natural order. For God to be truly divine He must be immutable (unchanging). God must remain a source of motion but still remain unmoved. If God did indeed move, He would be a changing Being—a mutable Being. All mutable beings have occasion not to be what they were—and might possibly not exist. God must always exist. There can never be an occasion where He can be what He was not before. God is the constant eternal Source of all motion, yet Immutable. And this First Source of motion (whether it be of that original motion as well as of succeeding motion) to be truly God must be distinguishable from any particular acts of motion and cannot be the result of any prior motion.

The premises in both the First and the Second Way presuppose two fundamental assumptions:

(i) *Things exist.* Like a Solipsist, even if we do not believe that an external world exists as a product of our mental functions, still things exist for us in that mental world. The denial that something exists is self-stultifying. There *must* be something existing. If the external world does not exist then at least the mental act exists of denying that an external world exists.

(ii) *Things change.* As Heracleitus (500 B.C.) put it: πάντα ρέι *"All things change."* And: *"You cannot step into the same river twice."* As the modern bumper sticker has it: *"Change is here to stay."* It is not essential to assume that all things change, only that there is change which among other ways can be described in terms of motion and/or causation.

There is no denying these two assumptions. They appear to be convincingly a posteriori or empirical. They seem to be facts of our experience of the world. But now let us examine in the next chapter each of the four premises and the conclusion using the Second Way as our guide.

III

God as the Temporal First Cause: The Uncaused Cause

3.1 The Second Way: The Argument From Causes. The serial, or "horizontal," feature of the argument may be presented thus:

(1) Everything that exists has a cause.

(2) And that cause has a cause (which has become the effect in relation to its prior cause). There is an order of efficient causes.

(3) Things are caused by other things and cannot be self-caused.

(4) These causes cannot go on ad infinitum into the past. They must stop somewhere at a First Cause. If there were an infinite regress of causes into the past, then nothing would have been begun to be caused at all and we would have no causes operating now—which we do have.

(5) There is a First Cause, an Uncaused Cause, who initially caused all things to begin moving, but is Himself uncaused by anything else. That we call God.

Aquinas' Second Way has basically the same argument form as the First Way. Most of the comments we will make about the First Cause also are applicable to the First Mover (Unmoved Mover, Prime Mover). Notice though the gradual shift in each argument from regarding motion and causes as agents capable of producing other motions and causes to the position that in order for things to be agents they must be acted upon by some Transnatural Being.

3.2   The First Premise: Does Everything That Exists Have a Cause?

It would be difficult if not impossible to dispute this first premise if it were stated in terms of the Principle of Causality: *Every event has a prior cause.* The Principle of Causality implies among other things:

(1) An event is a coming-into-existence of a thing.

(2) There are prior conditions called causes, which are constantly conjoined in a temporal succession to another event called the effect.

(3) These prior conditions (causes) are the necessary conditions for the occurrence of the effect, and in the absence of these prior conditions (causes) the effect will not occur.

(4) The existence of the same prior conditions (causes) is followed by the presence of the same effect. (Same cause, same effect.)

(5) Events in the Universe are causally related. (It is not necessary to assume, as does the Doctrine of Internal Relations, that any particular event is causally related to *all* other events. Any particular event is involved to some extent as a causal factor in other causally related events.)

(6) Any cause can be regarded as an *effect* of a previous event (cause) in a serial order.

(7) All events are caused. There are no uncaused events in the Universe. But as we shall see in a moment the Principle of Causality does not contradict the notion that there may be uncaused or noncaused things in the Universe such as eternally existing matter or energy.

(8) There are many events *for which causes are not* known but causes for these events can be found.

(9) There will always be some events to which causes have not as yet been assigned, or for which causes will not be known, but there are nevertheless causes for these events.

As it stands the first premise in Aquinas' argument ("Everything that exists has a cause") *could* be interpreted to mean that if a thing exists it must have a cause, and if it has a cause and only if it has a cause does it then exist. Under this interpretation one could argue that if God exists then He must have a cause, and if He has no cause then He cannot be said to exist. (What caused God to exist? What caused God to cause the First Cause, the First Motion?)

A distinction has to be made between statements such as:

(a) "Everything that exists must have a cause" and

(b) "Every act of coming-into-existence must have a cause."

An *event* (an identifiable something coming-into-existence) must have a cause. But it is not contradictory to hold that there is a class of things for which we need not assign a cause, *for it has no cause.* We can name this class the Eternal Universe or Matter, or, if we wish, God, Eternal Energy, Power, Force, or Eternal *Nous* (Cosmic Intelligence, The Universal Mind). We can even conceive of combinations of these *without their having a cause.* Whether they exist as they are specified as existing is another matter. But we shall see that *some* concept of an eternity of existence is as undeniable about reality as are such concepts as we discussed in the last chapter: *there is existence* (of some sort) and *there is change.*

If the Universe is eternal, then you can intelligibly talk about it as being *uncaused.* To ask for its cause would be nonsense. The Universe has no cause; it always existed. So with the concept of God, for assuredly God can be uncaused. If God is eternal, then He is uncaused. It would be silly then to ask "What caused God?" He just does not have a cause. Nor is there any need to assign a cause. But on the other hand it *is* contradictory to call God (or the Universe) an *Uncaused Cause.*

The Universe (matter, energy, substance, existence) may be uncaused, but any and every activity within it is caused—none of the events within it are uncaused. The Universe has an endless causal history. There is always a cause for the Universe being in the particular state of activity in which it is found. But this does not allow us to say that the Universe is an Uncaused Cause. The Universe is a collective noun that stands for "all that there is," and the Universe itself does not act in a causal fashion as the particular things within it do. If it did, there would be causes for its acting in that particular causal fashion. The concept of God could without inconsistency parallel this analysis of the Universe, but that would not make God an Uncaused Cause any more than the Universe is an Uncaused Cause of the events that happen within it.

As well, the concept of a First Cause is self-contradictory. If "cause" means what the second premise in Aquinas' argument tells us it means— that a cause is an effect of a previous cause, then we cannot have a

Cause, that is, a First Cause, since such a First Cause would *not* be a Cause—it is not the effect of a previous cause. The same applies to a First Movement. If the First Cause (or First Movement) to the Universe is an event, then it must have a previous cause—but it thus cannot be a First Cause since such a First Cause does not have a previous event preceding it. There is no sense in which a First Cause can meaningfully be called a Cause (or an event).

God indeed may be the Cause of that First Cause or First Movement, and we have thereby found a preceding cause or event to account for that First Cause. We now seem to be able to talk consistently about a First Cause—since there is a preceding cause to *it*. But even assuming the intelligibility of such a First Cause produced by God upon a Universe that was not previously causally related and active in time, we still must contend with an infinite regress of causes on another level: What caused God to cause *that* First Event, First Cause, First Movement in the Universe? When we find an answer to that question, then we have a further question of what caused that cause in God—ad infinitum. Now in this sense it is difficult if not impossible for God to be conceived as an *Uncaused Cause,* meaning that He *causes* things to happen without being caused to cause them. If God causes things to happen, if God acts, His activity cannot be noncaused, nor can it be noncausal. Both these phrases contradict the very meanings of activity and cause.

3.3   The Second Premise: Is There an Order of Efficient Causes?

We can talk about the cause of any and all particular events in the Universe. Theoretically we could trace the causal history of all events. But how do we determine a posteriori or empirically that "there is an *order* of efficient causes" in the world of sense? To find this "order of efficient causes" is a different search from finding the "efficient cause" of any particular thing. To talk about events being causally related is not to imply that they are causally interrelated in an overall ordered interconnection.

Aquinas' philosophy contained a reformulation of Aristotle's Four Causes. The following selection from Book II, chapter 3, of Aristotle's *Physics* explains his Four Causes:

> 3 . . . and men do not think they know a thing till they have grasped the "why" of it (which is to grasp its primary cause). So clearly we too must do this as regards both coming to be and passing away and every kind of physical change, in order that, knowing their principles, we may try to refer to these principles each of our problems.

In one sense, then, (1) that out of which a thing comes to be and which persists, is called "cause," e. g. the bronze of the statue, the silver of the bowl, and the genera of which the bronze and the silver are species.

In another sense (2) the form or the archetype, i.e. the statement of the essence, and its genera, are called "causes" (e.g. of the octave the relation of 2 : I, and generally number), and the parts in the definition.

Again (3) the primary source of the change or coming to rest; e.g. the man who gave advice is a cause, the father is cause of the child, and generally what makes of what is made and what causes change of what is changed.

Again (4) in the sense of end or "that for the sake of which" a thing is done, e.g. health is the cause of walking about. ("Why is he walking about?" we say. "To be healthy," and, having said that, we think we have assigned the cause.) The same is true also of all the intermediate steps which are brought about through the action of something else as means towards the end, e.g. reduction of flesh, purging, drugs, or surgical instruments are means towards health. All these things are "for the sake of" the end, though they differ from one another in that some are activities, others instruments.

This then perhaps exhausts the number of ways in which the term "cause" is used.[1]

We shall have more to say about these Four Causes and their implicitly theological character in chapter 7, "God as the Cosmic Mind." But what is important here is to point out that Aquinas took these Four Causes (*Material:* Of what stuff is the thing made? *Formal:* What form, idea, or essence does it have? *Efficient (Propelling):* What human agent, or natural set of conditions, made it? *Final (Telic):* For what purpose was it made, or what kind of thing will its completed stage be?) and interpreted them as one would the making of human artifacts. An artist makes the head of Zeus. The Material Cause is *marble.* The Efficient Cause is the energy applied over a period of time by the artist using his hammer and chisel. The Formal Cause is the form or idea of Zeus taking shape in the marble, which form or idea is in the mind of the artist which he is impressing

---

1. Originally published as *Physics,* trans. R. P. Hardie and R. K. Gaye, from *The Oxford Translation of Aristotle,* ed. W. D. Ross, vol. 2 (Oxford: The Clarendon Press, 1930), used by permission of The Clarendon Press, Oxford. Richard McKeon, ed., *The Basic Works of Aristotle* (New York: Random House, 1941), pp. 240–41. Used by permission of Random House.

upon the marble. The Final Cause is that final, end product for the sake of which the whole process takes place.

In the case of an artist, there is a transcendent teleological aspect to these Four Causes. The artist is in a sense separate from his medium. He gives his inner thought an objective reality in this medium. But Aristotle applies the Four Causes also to natural processes. This can be called the immanent teleological feature of the Four Causes. The Form and Matter are not separate except in abstraction. The reason for a thing's developing the way it does is not external to it but is integrally a part of the thing's own structures. An example would be an acorn developing into an oak tree or an embryo developing into a child. *The Material Cause:* This is the material stuff that the acorn or fetus is made of. *The Efficient Cause:* In the case of the acorn this is the wind, rain, soil, temperature. In the case of the fetus it is the complex changes surrounding the fetus in the mother's womb. *The Formal Cause:* This would be the form that the acorn and the child are developing into in the course of time in their development. The acorn will never become a child and the child never an oak tree. They have different "forms." *The Final Cause:* This is the τέλος or the end product—an oak tree from the acorn and a child from the embryo.

Aquinas stressed the *artifact* characteristics of the Four Causes. This implies the question "*Who made it?*" It leads to a Transcendent Being, a Supra- or Transnatural Being. The "order of efficient causes" is seen in terms of someone bringing them about to be what they are. They are brought to be as they are just as an artist brings about an order of efficient causes to produce an artifact. Had Aquinas stressed the immanent teleological feature of the Four Causes when he applied them in his arguments his conception of God and Nature would have been somewhat different.

Now while we may grant that each and every artifact and natural object does have an efficient cause, Aristotle's account did not render necessary that there be a cause (an efficient cause) of *those* operating causes—which is what Aquinas assumes. This second premise still leaves us with the question: *Is there an Order of efficient causes?* Is it necessary to assume a Cause (God) of efficient or even final causes which exists in the world?

We may mention in passing that Aristotle's Final and Formal Causes have been subject to considerable criticism by philosophers who do not believe them to be operative in the world. Also Aristotle's Four Causes do not provide us with what might be called a "descriptive causality" in a modern scientific sense. Aristotle's word αἰτία (aitia) meant "cause" in the sense of presenting all the possible ways we could *talk about* how things come to be the way they are—how they develop from a beginning process to a completed state. These αἰτίαι (causes) are the *reasons* that can be given in language for the temporal development of *all classes of change* from potentiality to actuality. Linguistically they have been applied as "causal explanations" to any and all situations but they do not present a causal description of any specific operating changes, which is what modern scientific explanation demands.

3.4 The Third Premise: Can Things Be Self-Caused?

The concept of "self-caused" is self-contradictory. As Aquinas puts it: "There is no case known (neither is it, indeed, possible) in which a thing is found to be the efficient cause of itself; for so it would be prior to itself, which is impossible." If the thing were *prior to itself* in order to cause itself, then it need not cause itself since it is already in existence. If the thing were *not* prior to itself in order to cause its existence, then something *else* must have been in existence to bring it into existence—and such a happening is *not self-causation.*

We can apply this line of reasoning to show what Aquinas himself believed, that God is not—and cannot be—"self-caused." If we assume that everything has a cause, we then might ask, "What caused God?" We can answer in at least three possible ways, the first two of which are unsatisfactory:

(1) God was caused by a Cause existing before Him. This leads us into an Infinite Regress of Gods. That kind of serial polytheism is unsatisfactory to monotheism.

(2) God is self-caused. Nothing caused Him. He caused Himself.This is as logically impossible as "a *thing causing itself.*" If God caused Himself, then He must have existed to cause Himself. But if He already existed then He did not have to cause Himself to exist. And if He did *not* exist prior to Himself to cause Himself, then where did God come from? We then still have the question we began with: "What caused God?"

(3) This third alternative we have already discussed in 3.2. God is Eternal. He is not caused by anything else. There never was a time at which God was not. He always has been. Thus if God is Eternal, the question "What caused God?" is meaningless. That sort of question doesn't apply to something that is *eternal.* It applies only to things that come-to-be and pass-away which God does not do. But what could God be like if He does not come-to-be and pass-away?

That God does not come-to-be-and-pass-away is a belief older than Plato. This was one meaning of "eternal." Something eternal cannot be in change or process. Something eternal must be permanent, unchanging, and, in the case of God, Perfect. If something is eternal in these senses then it is divine. The truly eternal cannot-not-be what it is and then come-to-be what it is and again come-not-to-be what it was. We shall have occasion to examine this more closely later.

There is another conception of eternal that is found in the Greek Atomists. The Universe is composed of a finite (or infinite if you wish) number of kinds of atoms which are eternal without Beginning or End, and which are permanent and do not change. They themselves do not undergo any process of "coming-into-being-and-passing-away." These atoms combine and redistribute according to their shape and motions to form the configurations and patterns that temporarily exist in the Universe. The atoms themselves are the building blocks but they remain eternally the same. Everything else which is formed by them passes-away at some time or another in Eternity.

But there is still another conception of eternal that is logically possible. A short presentation of it here may be helpful for our analysis in later sections. It is possible to conceive of an Eternality of "comings-into-being" and "passing-aways" without anything at all remaining eternally the same, or permanent, or unchanging. Nothing in this Eternity of Time would be the same as it was at some previous time—no matter how old it was, or how long it remained the same. That is, you could always find a time in this Eternity at which that thing could be seen to be different from what it was at another time. This would be an Eternal Universe in which not even Matter or Energy itself over periods of time would remain as it was at some previous time. This notion of eternal holds that *something or other Exists at any moment in Eternal Time* as opposed to *Something Exists Eternally* without changing.

3.5 *Must the Universe Itself Have a Cause?* If everything in the Universe has a cause does the Universe itself have a cause?

The *fallacy of composition* consists in arguing that what is true about some or all of the parts of a whole is also true of the whole itself. For example, an Eskimo murders a Mountie. We then conclude that Eskimos are murderers. All the members of the team are married. We then conclude that the team itself has a wife.

Sometimes this way of arguing is correct. But its correctness does not depend on its logical form. It depends on whether or not it is in fact the case that the whole does indeed also possess the quality of the parts. "All the members of this community are millionaires. The community itself is wealthy." This could very well be correct. To determine whether or not it is correct we would have to define what community is and show in what way it is wealthy (which word may have another meaning when applied to community).

We can see how the fallacy of composition applies in the case of the Universe. Because everything in the Universe has a cause, it does not mean that the Universe itself has this characteristic of having a cause. The Universe could very well be an Uncaused, Eternal, Infinite Regress of causes and events without beginning.

Each and every member of the Universe could have a different cause, yet the entire collection of these members (the Universe) need not have any cause for it.

3.6 Is the Universe a "Thing"? It is hardly possible not to call anything we can give a name to a "thing." (The word Universe does not appear to be an exception to this.) "Thing" may be applied to objects existing outside our inner reality of thinking and imagining. But there is nothing in our language preventing us from calling anything in our inner reality a "thing." Spirits, ghosts, angels, emotions—anything that can be named can have the word "thing" attached to it—that spirit "thing," that "thing" we all call a ghost.

This is related to two problems: The first is that of "hypostatization" (sometimes called "reification"). Because we can name something or have an idea of it, we tend to assign an objective existence to it. We have a name and an idea for the concepts 'beauty', 'good', 'nation'. They must exist as external realities around which we internalize our conceptions of them. They must exist in some way as external to our subjective conceptualizations of them in order to "produce" these concepts in us, and in order to "produce" the external reality of these concepts which we recognize.

An extreme paradigm of hypostatization is Plato's Theory of Forms. There is a realm in another world of Perfect Beauty, Perfect Goodness, Perfect Straightness. Every and all examples of beauty in this world are imperfect imitations of these Perfect Ideas existing in a self-subsisting and eternal way. We could never recognize a particular beautiful thing unless we had some intimate knowledge in some way of this Perfect Beauty to which we can compare a particular object and judge the extent to which that object is beautiful. These Perfect Ideas may not directly cause the existence of particular things, but their very existence serves as the Ideal Type to which objects in the Universe aspire to become with an innate Love. (This last point is a simple way of stating one of the Greek meanings of Uncaused Cause.)

The word "Universe" is a collective noun. It is a collection of things. It itself is not to be regarded as a "thing" in the sense that things in this collection are "things." It is not to be reified or hypostatized into a substantive and causal entity that exists apart from its meaning. The word "Universe" stands for that unique collection which is *Everything That There Is.*

The second problem is a problem of meaning. If a word applies in the same respect to any and all situations then its meaning is vacuous. If there is nothing to which I cannot apply the word "thing" then what is its signification? Everything and anything is a referent for it and it loses its specific meaning. Its "meaning" then consists in the possibility of applying it to anything at all. Any meaning for it can only come from the meaning of the concept, or referent, to which we are attaching the word "thing." We encounter this type of problem with reference to such words as "existence." What is *not* an existence of some sort? We can though in very abstract and general terms make a conceptual distinction between "inner" and "outer" existence. Other words that fall into this class are whole, part, being, becoming, potentiality, actuality.

The word "Universe" does not fall into this category of being which is essentially vacuous for it does not apply to *any* and *every* particular "thing" but to "all the classes of things that are"—it means "All that there is." The word is not vacuous but it is Total, All-Inclusive, Comprehensive. In this sense it cannot have characteristics applied to it which are applied to those other things which are labelled Existence, Whole, Being, Becoming. We may still call the Universe a Thing, but it cannot have any of the characteristics ascribed to other "things."

3.7   What Does "Everything That There Is" Mean?

(1) "Everything that there is" may mean that the Universe is a Whole—its items are finite in number at any given moment.

"Whole" with reference to the Universe may mean

(a) the sum-total of these items and nothing more. Parts interact with other parts without any overall organizing influence from the "Whole."

"Whole" may also mean,

(b) that sum-total plus some kind of operating presence whereby this "Whole" exerts an influence upon its parts—parts interact with other parts within the whole to fulfill the function, purpose, volition of that whole.

We encounter special difficulties on both interpretations of "Whole." In the first case, what is beyond this finite whole? Nothing at all. An "Infinity of Nothingness." If the Universe is Finite—a determinable "Whole" in either sense (a) or (b)—why must there be an Infinite Being as its Cause? Why—if a Cause is insisted upon—cannot this Cause also be a Finite Being or Whole? This is an issue separate from the problem of what can the phrase Infinite Being mean. For a Being to have characteristics and to be a causal agent, it cannot be Infinite for any concept of an Infinite would preclude the possibility of its acting as a concerted Whole. What would "Infinite Being" mean in the phrase "An Infinite Being caused the Universe which is a Whole"?

In the second sense of "Whole" the word "Whole" takes on an animistic character. It is the picture-concept of the Universe as a deliberate and conscious agent willing things to happen and organizing them according to thoughts. We don't see bricks, cement, sand, and water coming together to form a house. Parts are put together with other parts in an organized way according to a volition in order to bring together a house.

Again we are committing the *fallacy of composition* if we jump to the conclusion that the Universe itself acts consciously this way as a Whole. Certainly there are many results in our part of the solar system that are due to conscious willing and deliberation. But this need not mean that *all* arrangements of order have this as their source, nor does it mean that the Universe itself must as a Whole possess this characteristic of volition or conscious deliberation which a part of it possesses.

It seems that "Whole" with reference to the Universe can only mean "the sum-total." If the word "Whole" as applied to the Universe is interpreted in the second sense (b) as something over and above its "sum-total" of items, then we run up against a special problem which could go like this: You are a stranger to the English language, you are visiting here and a friend invites you to see his room. He shows you his guitar, his Playboy pictures on the walls, his oriental carpet, and his artistic chandeliers in which he hides his bourbon. He has finished thoroughly itemizing the objects in his room. Your friend then asks you, "How do you like my room?" But you turn to your friend and say: "I haven't seen it yet. Where is it? I've seen most everything in the room, thank you, but now show me the 'room' that you were going to show me."

There is no "room" over and above the particulars that can be enumerated and the space that can be located within the walls. "Room" is a word that stands very abstractly for a group of things but has no objective, substantial existence as do the things for which it is a collective noun. "Universe" is a word that stands even more abstractly for the collection of all things that have existence, but It itself is not a particular subsisting existence like each individual thing in it.

If the word "Whole" as applied to the Universe is interpreted in the second sense (b) as something over and above its sum-total of items, we then face another related problem. We will tend to assume some version of "The whole is greater than the sum of its parts." Quantitatively this can never be correct for the simple reason that by definition the whole *must be equal* to the sum of its parts. But let us allow that in some qualitative way the whole is greater than the sum of its parts. The human mind, human actions, the psyche possibly can be thought of as being something over and above the sum total of our bodily parts when acting as a whole. Now while this may work with qualitative wholes in the Universe, this argument cannot work when applied to the Universe as a Whole—and the *only* Whole that exists.

These qualitative functions that are claimed to be over and above the sum-total are dependent upon and interrelated with other wholes and parts and items in the Universe in order to be what they are. If the Universe is defined as "All that there is" then there would be nothing outside it to interrelate with in order to produce these functions that are "over and above" the sum-total. We are back again to the Universe being a sum-total in the first sense (a). (That is, *if* it is a sum-total. It could be Infinite, thus not a Whole, and thus not a sum-total.)

If we postulate God, or some kind of Being, which interrelated with the Universe as a Whole to produce these "over and above" qualities, then we have this difficulty: If 'Universe' means *"All that there is"* and God *Is*, then God must be included in the "All that there is." He then becomes a member of the unique collection "All that there is." The question then remains: Is there such a member? What is He like? But this in no way alters the position that the Universe is a sum-total in the sense (a) and *not* in the sense (b) of there being an over-and-above quality to it.

We could suppose the word "Universe" to mean "all that there is— excluding God." God stands in relation to "All that there is—the Universe." This changes our meaning of the word "Universe." This is no drastic problem. Up to a point we can define words arbitrarily and ignore conventional usage. But still our main problems do not go away. Is there such a Being that stands in relation to "All that there is"? What is that relationship? If it is different from what there is, then how can it be known or shown?

(2) But "everything that there is" may mean that the Universe is *not* a Whole, but is an *Infinite Collection*. If the Universe is an Infinite Collection and is eternal it would be unintelligible to assign a Moment in time at which such an Infinite Collection was brought into being by a separate Being—even if that Being Itself were Infinite.

3.8   The Fourth Premise: Is an Infinite Regress of Causes (or Motions) Possible? The fourth premise which denies an Infinite Regress contradicts the first three premises. We have already seen that for Aquinas when we look around we find that things are causally related. There exists an order of (efficient) causality. Nothing can be its own efficient cause. To be one's own efficient cause is to be other than oneself in order to be the efficient cause which is an impossible state of affairs. Thus since each thing is caused it must be caused by some other thing, and that by something else, and that by something else. But there cannot be an Infinite Regress of causes. There must be a First Term in the series. Why? Because the ordered series of causes would not be completed and there would not have been any causes started. To get the ordered series of causes started there must have been a First Efficient Cause which is itself not caused which got the ordered series of causes going in the first place. Unless the series of causes (or motions) has an Absolute Beginning-point before which there were no previous causes or motions, then nothing could ever have begun to change. There would be nothing going on Now or at Anytime.

Requoting from Aquinas' Second Way:

> Now in efficient causes it is not possible to go on to infinity, because in all efficient causes following in order, the first is the cause of the intermediate cause, and the intermediate is the cause of the ultimate cause, whether the intermediate cause be several or one only. Now to take away the cause is to take away the effect. Therefore, if there be no first cause among efficient causes, there will be no ultimate, nor any intermediate, cause. But if in efficient causes it is possible to go on to infinity, there will be no first efficient cause, neither will there be an ultimate effect, nor any intermediate

efficient causes; all of which is plainly false. Therefore it is necessary
to admit a first efficient cause, to which everyone gives the name
of God.[2]

We can see how Aquinas was influenced by passages from Aristotle's
philosophy such as:

> 2 But evidently there *is* a first principle, and the causes of things
> are neither an infinite series nor infinitely various in kind. For (1)
> neither can one thing proceed from another, as from matter, *ad
> infinitum* (e.g. flesh from earth, earth from air, air from fire, and
> so on without stopping), nor can the sources of movement form
> an endless series (man for instance being acted on by air, air by
> the sun, the sun by strife, and so on without limit). Similarly the
> final causes cannot go on *ad infinitum*—walking being for the sake
> of health, this for the sake of happiness, happiness for the sake
> of something else, and so on one thing always for the sake of
> another. And the case of the essence is similar. For in the case
> of intermediates, which have a last term and a term prior to them,
> the prior must be the cause of the later terms. For if we had to
> say which of the three is the cause, we should say the first; surely
> not the last, for the final term is the cause of none; nor even the
> intermediate, for it is the cause only of one. (It makes no difference
> whether there is one intermediate or more, nor whether they are
> infinite or finite in number.) But of series which are infinite in
> this way, and of the infinite in general, all the parts down to that
> now present are alike intermediates; so that if there is no first there
> is no cause at all.[3]

> . . . But if there is nothing eternal, neither can there be a process
> of coming to be; for there must be something that comes to be,
> i.e. from which something comes to be, and the ultimate term in
> this series cannot have come to be, since the series has a limit
> and since nothing can come to be out of that which is not. Further,
> if generation and movement exist there must also be a limit; for
> no movement is infinite, but every movement has an end, and that
> which is incapable of completing its coming to be cannot be in
> process of coming to be; and that which has completed its coming
> to be must *be* as soon as it has come to be. Further, since the matter
> exists, because it is ungenerated, it is *a fortiori* reasonable that the
> substance or essence, that which the matter is at any time coming
> to be, should exist, for if neither essence nor matter is to be, nothing

---

2. Anton C. Pegis, ed., *Introduction to St. Thomas Aquinas* (New York: Random House,
1967), *Summa Theologica*, Q. 2, Art. 3, pp. 24-27. Used by permission of the publisher.

3. Ibid., p. 713.

will be at all, and since this is impossible there must be something besides the concrete thing, viz. the shape or form.⁴

    Aquinas' arguments denying the possibility of an infinite series of events (causes, motions, beginnings) temporally linked together into the past may be presented in several ways. Here is one way: Events are Now occurring. No one can deny this fundamental truth. Of course you may not be able precisely to pin-point any Now. Everytime you try to do so it is a Now that has passed and never a Now that is present. Nor is a future event a Now yet. Nevertheless we all know there is a Now—Now! "Now" is fundamental to all thought as well as to having a thought.

    We also all know, and it is undeniable, that every event no matter how short takes some time to occur—the flutter of a bee's wings, the movement of an electron, light coming from a source. No matter how short each event may be, *an infinite series of them will take an infinite amount of time to get through.* If an infinite series of events has passed before this Now event, then an infinite amount of time also has been passed through before this Now event could come about. But if an infinite amount of time and an infinite amount of events had to be gone through before the Now, we would not have arrived at the Now since an infinite series would have to be gone through. We all know that a Now is here, therefore only a finite amount of time, and a finite number of events could have preceded this present Now event. The series prior to the Now can only be finite. There cannot be an Infinite Regress.

    Kant presented this form of argument in the Thesis part of the First Four Antimonies. Each of the Four Antimonies (a Beginning to the Universe; a Simple Substance; Freedom of the Will; a Necessary Being) were Theses of what Kant called *rationalistic metaphysics.* Each of the theses could be contrasted with an antithesis from the empirical-scientific viewpoint. Kant believed that solid arguments could be found for both the Theses and for the Antitheses. All of the eight defenses in Kant are *reductio ad absurdum* arguments.

    The Thesis in the First Antimony is that the world *does* have a Beginning in Time (and also is spatially limited). The Antithesis is that the world has *no* Beginning in Time (and is not spatially limited) but is Infinite in Time (and Infinite in Space).

THESIS

The world has a beginning in time, and is limited also with regard to space.

---

4. Ibid., p. 724.

Proof

For if we assumed that the world had no beginning in time, then
an eternity must have elapsed up to every given point of time,
and therefore an infinite series of successive states of things must
have passed in the world. The infinity of a series, however, consists
in this, that it never can be completed by means of a successive
synthesis. Hence an infinite past series of worlds is impossible,
and the beginning of the world a necessary condition of its existence.[5]

When Kant uses such phrases as "an eternity must have elapsed,"
and "therewith passed away an infinite series of successive states," he
clearly is being caught up in the pictorial and definitional contradictions
of phrases we freely use in ordinary language about infinity, such as,
"stretching back to infinity"; "approaching the Infinite"; "going on back
to the Infinite." If we are not careful these phrases can easily make
us imply that there is something infinitely back there to which we can
"stretch" or "approach" or "go." 'Infinity' is not a thing, object, or point
to which anything can go. It is a process or function. These phrases
work on two levels: the pictorial and the linguistic (the definitional).
The two levels are incongruent and contradictory. We are "seeing"
something different from that which we are "saying." So with Kant's
phrase "an eternity must have elapsed." By *definition* an eternity of events
stretching into the past *cannot* elapse—otherwise it could not be an Eternal
Series. *By definition* an infinite series cannot have "passed away."

The infinite regress argument is consistent and argues in this way:
It is only impossible to "pass through" an infinite series of events in
a *finite* amount of time. If Time is infinite, then there would be enough
Time in the past for all the infinite series to have occurred before the
present Now. It is *not* contradictory to hold that an Infinite Series of
events into the past has a present Now event. An Infinite Series of
events can be Infinite into the past despite the fact that an end, or
completion point, Now, exists. All that is being asserted is that the Infinite
Series of events has no end, no Beginning Point at a Time past from
any Now—*no matter when that Now is designated*. No matter how many
events in the Series stretching into the past are named, there will always
be at least one that is there but has not as yet been named.

The moment any Now is designated as a member in the Infinite Series
stretching into the past, it becomes a *member* of the (Infinite) Series
stretching into the Future. But this designated member does not presup-

---

5. Theodore Meyer Greene, ed., *Kant Selections* (New York: Charles Scribner's Sons,
1929), pp. 189–90. Used by permission of the publisher.

pose that an Infinite Series has already been completed. *Each* and *every* member in the Infinite Series ends, or is completed, but the Infinite Series into the past itself has no end, and is not completed. There is no member in the Infinite Series which is not an elapsed member, but the Infinite Series is not a member to elapse. The events in the Infinite Series are completed but the Infinite Time and the Infinite Series are never completed.

The Infinite Series stretching into the past has an end or completion only in the sense that there is one member in the Infinite Series, namely the designated Now after which there are no more as yet designated members. Any and all designated members that have already passed serve as a condition for knowing the possibility of an Infinite Series. None of this implies an end or completion of the Infinite Series in the sense of any "successive synthesis." Nor does it imply them in the sense of any "successive addition" into a *sum* of its members.

The kind of criticism we are presenting of the Infinite Series into the Past tends to picture an *Event* which must have happened an Infinite Time ago. It then presupposes that between that Event and a Now, there *cannot* be an Infinite Series, but there must be a Finite number of events (though exceedingly large).

But the infinite regress argument holds that *no Event happened an Infinite Time ago.* This would be a contradiction in terms. There is an Infinite Series of events stretching backwards. No two members of the Infinite Series are an infinite distance apart in the Series. All members of the Infinite Series are at finite distances apart. The Series itself is an Infinite Series but the distance between any two members is always *finite.* Another way of putting this is that however far apart two events in the Series are from each other you will always find

(1) events that are still further apart than *they* are and

(2) from any given past event there will be an Infinite number of previous events to that event.

The First Cause argument insists that without a *First* Beginning-Point to the series—without the series being finite—it would be impossible for there to be anything in existence Now. On the contrary, the infinite regress argument insists that with the series being *infinite* it would be possible for things to be in existence Now since there would always have been a causal series in existence with no First member and no need for a First Cause with the attendant contradictions. To quote from Hans Reichenbach (1891–1953):

To ask how matter was generated from nothing, or to ask for a first cause, in the sense of a cause of the first event, or of the universe as a whole, is not a meaningful question. Explanation in terms of causes means pointing out a previous event that is connected with the latter event in terms of general laws. If there were a first event, it could not have been a cause, and it would not be meaningful to ask for an explanation. But there need not have been a first event; we can imagine that every event was preceded by an earlier event, and that time has no beginning. The infinity of time, in both directions, offers no difficulties to the understanding. We know that the series of numbers has no end, that for every number there is a larger number. If we include the negative numbers, the number series has no beginning either; for every number there is a smaller number. Infinite series without a beginning and an end have been successfully treated in mathematics; there is nothing paradoxical in them. To object that there must have been a first event, a beginning of time, is the attitude of an untrained mind. . . .

It has become a favorite argument of antiscientific philosophies that explanation must stop somewhere, that there remains unanswerable questions. But the questions so referred to are constructed by a misuse of words. Words meaningful in one combination may be meaningless in another. Could there be a father who never had a child? Everyone would ridicule a philosopher who regarded this question as a serious problem. The question of the cause of the first event, or of the cause of the universe as a whole, is not of a better type. The word "cause" denotes a relation between two things and is inapplicable if only one thing is concerned. The universe as a whole has no cause, since, by definition, there is no thing outside it that could be its cause. Questions of this type are empty verbalisms rather than philosophic arguments.[6]

3.9   The Conclusion (5): There Is a First Cause. The First Cause regarded either as a natural event or as a transnatural event involves contradictions. We have already seen the contradictory features in the notion of a Cause or Event before which there is no preceding Cause or Event. The meanings of "Cause" and "Event" imply previous conditions. It is not a matter of wondering what we are to look for when we talk about a Natural First Cause before which there are no prior Events, but a matter of our *never* being able to find such a thing since it is a contradiction in terms.

Here is another way of showing the contradictory nature of a First Cause: Can we in Time come to a First Cause which would be the

---

6. Hans Reichenbach, *The Rise of Scientific Philosophy* (Berkeley and Los Angeles: University of California Press, 1951), pp. 207–8. Originally published by the University of California Press; reprinted by permission of The Regents of the University of California.

First Member of the whole temporal series of causes? If we can do this then that Event, that First Cause (First Member), was an event in Time. Every time is conditioned by a previous time. That is, there is no time which has no preceding time to it. (There is no moment, or event in time, that does not have a previous moment in time.) There is no sense in the question "At what time did Time begin," which is what we might ask if we thought in terms of a "Beginning" of Time. Thus we must assume an infinite regress of time which itself assumes an infinite regress of events happening in that time since Time can only be known and made intelligible in terms of events happening at a time, or "in" a time.

This is perhaps an overly sophisticated way of pointing out that if we ever did find a First Cause we could intelligibly ask "What caused It?" And if that is found: "What caused It? "—ad infinitum in a sequence into the past. And there need be no jump into something which transends this natural realm.

The First Cause argument for God's existence itself does not prove that there is a Transnatural Being. It presupposes such a Transnatural Being in its premises. Neither does it prove that there is a single First Cause (God). It does not establish the present existence of such a First Cause (God). It does not show that this First Cause (God) is a Transnatural God who possesses the attributes of Love, Mercy, Perfection, Omniscience, Omnipotence, Omnibenevolence, and so on.

If the First Cause or First Mover can be accepted as a Transnatural Being standing outside the Universe then we run into a few other problems:

(1) If the First Cause (God) is transnatural and yet is like ordinary natural causes and motions, then in what respects is It a *Trans*natural Cause? To the extent that it is active as a First Cause to that extent it would have to be understood as a Natural rather than a Transnatural Being.

(2) If the First Cause, or First Mover, is transnatural and unlike ordinary causes and motions, then how could It be known? Such a Transnatural Being would be different from ordinary causes and motions and it would be difficult, if not impossible, to give it sense by calling it a "Cause" or "Mover." We can understand the concepts of "cause" or "mover" when applied to particular existing things, but if they don't mean the same thing when applied to God, whatever could they mean? And when they do mean the same when applied to God, we get anthropomorphism.

IV

God as the Creator Ex Nihilo

4.1 Introduction. We have discussed the temporal, serial or horizontal aspect of Aquinas' first two Ways. We will consider the vertical, or ultimate ground, aspect of those two arguments in the next chapter on "God as the Necessary Being: The Sustaining Cause of Change." In this chapter we want to analyze the notion of God as Creator. God as Creator has been thought of as a Force using pre-existing material, shaping it into what we have. God as Creator has been thought of as that upon which all things utterly depend for their existence. We shall not in the main be concerned with the variations of these notions since they are similar in conception to the material we have covered and will be covering. In this chapter, beginning with section two, we want to limit our presentation to God's Creation of the Universe *ex nihilo—out of nothing.*

There are four creation beliefs in our Greek-Hebrew-Christian traditions which are not ex nihilo conceptions: the Begetter, the Emission, the Emanation, and the Artisan.

> (1) The *Begetter* conception of God's Creation is found in popular Greek and early popular Hebrew religions. Creation is described in an analogy with the natural procreation of animal life, or of man himself.

There is a long and persistent attempt in the history of Greek-Hebrew-Christian thought to deny this biological procreative analogy

45

as applied to God's Creation of the Universe. Here is one of the many examples which can be given of such denials from the early Church Fathers who grappled with this Begetter notion of Creation. They were especially concerned since the birth of Jesus from the Virgin Mary could be so construed by the uninitiated:

> . . . —not as the poets and mythographers describe sons of gods begotten of sexual union, but as the truth describes the Logos, always innate in the heart of God. For before anything else came into existence he had this as his Counsellor, his own Mind and Intelligence. When God wished to make what he had planned to make, he generated this Logos, making him external, as the *firstborn of all creation* (Col. 1:15). He did not deprive himself of the Logos but generated the Logos and constantly converses with his Logos. Hence the holy scriptures and all those inspired by the Spirit teach us, and one of them, John, says, "In the beginning was the Logos, and the Logos was with God" (John 1:1). He shows that originally God was alone and the Logos was in him. Then he says, "And the Logos was God; everything was made through him, and apart from him nothing was made" (John 1:1-3). Since the Logos is God and derived his nature from God, whenever the Father of the universe wills to do so he sends him into some place where he is present and is heard and seen. He is sent by God and is present in a place.[1]

The Church Fathers toiled relentlessly to find an adequate language to overcome reproductive meanings for their terms, while still explaining such things as the "sonship" of Jesus (ὁ μονογενής—the only begotten Son: John 1:18); the "first born"(πρωτότοκος Col. 1:15); and the "Fatherhood" of God. They attempted to use such words as ἀποκοπή (abscission); γεννηθέντα (generated); ἐκπορευόμενον (proceeding from); πέμψω (I will send); ἐφάνη or ἔδειξε (as one who was made to appear, or to be, manifested or shown); κτίσμα (as a created being); προελθών (coming forth); προπηδα (springs forth); πεφυκώς (naturally produced); προβολή(prolation); προβλήθεις (emission); κατὰ μερισμόν (according to separation—or by participation, depending on the context); μετέχεσθαι (to be participated).

With the pressure to codify the Christian viewpoint and make it conceptually acceptable and consistent, the Second Ecumenical Conference (381 A.D.) at Constantinople officially used the term γεννηθέτα

---

1. Robert M. Grant, trans., *Theophilus of Antioch ad Autolycum* (London: Oxford University Press, 1970), pp. 63–65. Copyright 1970 Oxford University Press and used by permission of the Clarendon Press, Oxford. The Greek word in this passage translated as "generated" is ἐγέννησεν. It means "gave birth to."

(generated, or having been born). This was to be used in connection with the coming-into-being of the Son, Jesus or the Logos. The term ἐκπορευόμενον (proceeding from) was officially to be used in connection with the coming-into-being of the Holy Spirit. This controversy still continues.

(2) The *Emission* theory of God's Creation is found mostly among the Greek and Roman Stoics. The Universe is itself a living thing with a Soul. The sum total of all our human souls is part of the Universal Soul. God is the *Logos* (λόγος) or "seminal reason" (λόγος σπερματικός) of the Universe.

Diogenes Laertius describes this viewpoint:

> The doctrine that the world is a living being, rational, animate and intelligent, is laid down by Chrysippus in the first book of his treatise *On Providence,* by Apollodorus in his *Physics,* and by Posidonius. It is a living thing in the sense of an animate substance endowed with sensation; for animal is better than non-animal, and nothing is better than the world, *ergo* the world is a living being. And it is endowed with soul, as is clear from our several souls being each a fragment of it.[2]

> God is one and the same with Reason, Fate, and Zeus; he is also called by many other names. In the beginning he was by himself; he transformed the whole of substance through air into water, and just as in animal generation the seed has a moist vehicle, so in cosmic moisture God, who is the seminal reason of the universe, remains behind in the moisture as such an agent, adapting matter to himself with a view to the next stage of creation. Thereupon he created first of all the four elements, fire, water, air, earth. They are discussed by Zeno in his treatise *On the Whole,* by Chrysippus in the first book of his *Physics,* and by Archedemus in a work *On Elements.* An element is defined as that from which particular things first come to be at their birth and into which they are finally resolved. The four elements together constitute unqualified substance or matter.[3]

> The world, in their view, is ordered by reason and providence; so says Chrysippus in the fifth book of his treatise *On Providence* and Posidonius in his work *On the Gods,* book iii.—inasmuch as

---

2. R. D. Hicks, trans., *Diogenes Laertius* (Cambridge, Mass.: Harvard University Press, 1958), vol. II, p. 247. Used by permission of the publisher.

3. Ibid., p. 241.

reason pervades every part of it, just as does the soul in us. Only there is a difference of degree; in some parts there is more of it, in others less. For through some parts it passes as a "hold" or containing force, as is the case with our bones and sinews; while through others it passes as intelligence, as in the ruling part of the soul. Thus, then, the whole world is a living being, endowed with soul and reason, and having aether for its ruling principle . . . .[4]

(3) The *Emanation* conception of God's Creation uses the analogy of the sun and its light. The sun is the source of light. Light "emanates" from the sun and is dependent upon it but is not identical with it. If we take away the sun, we take away light. The further from the sun we get the less brightness of the light. So with God. God is the Source (the Generator) of the Universe. All things Emanate from God and are dependent upon God but are not identical with God. Take away God, we take away the Universe. The further away from God a thing is the less spirituality it possesses. Matter is the furthest away from God, and Pure Spirit is the closest. The Emanation theory is not Pantheism. It is a version of Panentheism. (All things are *in* God who is their Source and from Whom all things proceed. All things are part of the identity of God but are *hierarchically* "Other than the First.") Pantheism is: *All is God. God is All.* The Universe and God are two different names for the same thing. God and the Universe are *identical.*

We are not discussing Pantheism as one of the Creator theories since strictly speaking there is no Creator involved. There is only the Universe in which creations—things coming-into-being—occur.

Pan-Psychism is the belief that God is the Psyche, Spirit, or Form totally immanent *in Matter*, or the Universe operating upon it as its Guiding Principle. God is not to be identified with Matter, or the Universe, but with that Psychic Force in Matter with which it is totally and Eternally integrated.

Spinoza (1632–1677) has been called a Pantheist but his philosophy is also at times Panentheistic and at other

4. Ibid., p. 243.

times Pan-Psychistic. The Emission theory (2) where the
Universe is seen as a living organic whole is akin to
Pantheism.

Plotinus (205-270) is the best Neo-Platonic proponent
of the Emanation concept:

The law of necessary production: each Principle must eternally
produce the level of being immediately below it as a necessary
consequence of its own existence; and the whole order of things
is eternal: the lower world of becoming was not created at a particular moment but is eternally being generated: it is always there as
a whole, and particular things in it only perish so that others may
come into being.

Each must give of its own being to something else. The Good
will not be the Good, or *Nous, Nous;* Soul will not be itself, unless
after the primal life some secondary life lives as long as the primal
exists. All things must exist for ever in ordered dependence upon
each other: those other than the First have come into being only
in the sense of being derived and dependent. Things that are said
to have come into being did not just come into being (at a particular
moment) but always were and always will be in process of becoming;
nor does anything perish except what can be transformed into
something else; that which has nothing into which it can be transformed does not perish.[5]

(The One transcends being because it is its source, *Nous* proceeds
from the One, and Soul from *Nous*, by a double movement of
outgoing and return in contemplation, the higher in each case
remaining in itself, unaffected by the production of the lower. Soul
in its turn produces another level of being or hypostasis, Nature,
the Life-Principle.)

The One is all things and not a single one of them: for the Source
of all is not all things; yet It is all things, for they all, so to speak,
run back to It: or, rather, in It they are not yet, but will be. How
then do all things come from the One, Which is simple and has
in It no diverse variety, or any sort of doubleness? It is because
there is nothing in It that all things come from It: in order that
being may exist, the One is not being but the Generator of being.
This, we may say, is the first act of generation. The One, perfect
because It seeks nothing, has nothing, and needs nothing overflows,
as it were, and Its superabundance makes something other than
Itself. This, when it has come into being, turns back upon the One
and is filled, and so becomes Its contemplator, *Nous.* Its halt and

---

5. A. H. Armstrong, trans., *Plotinus* (London: Allen & Unwin, 1953), pp. 53. Used by
permission of the publisher.

turning towards the One constitutes being, its gaze upon the One, *Nous*. Since it halts and turns towards the One that it may see, it becomes at once *Nous* and being. Resembling the One thus, *Nous* produces in the same way, pouring forth a multiple power. Just as That, Which was before it, poured forth its likeness, so what *Nous* produces is a likeness of itself. This activity springing from being is Soul, which comes into being while *Nous* abides unchanged: for *Nous* too comes into being while That which is before it abides unchanged.[6]

(4) The *Artisan* conception of God's Creation is based on the analogy of an artist with his work. The artist has an idea for a work of art in his mind. He sets about putting his idea into the medium he is using. The medium itself which he is using imposes limitations upon his ability in executing his idea as it is in his mind. He cannot fully express the idea as it is in itself, or as it exists in his mind. He can only be content with an approximate image or imitation of it.

So with God. God is that Rational Power attempting to imprint His Plan, Design, Ideas upon an Eternally active Material Universe, or a Chaos. He brings a Pattern and Order into the Universe which has a "Necessity" of its own. And this Pattern and Order is towards the Good (towards the Best of All Possible Worlds under the circumstances), and towards the Beautiful, and the Just and the Truth. Nothing is done by God without a Reason. Nothing happens in the Universe without its having a reason for its happening in that way rather than another (Principle of Sufficient Reason).

Plato is one of the early proponents of this Artisan view of God's Creation and all such conceptions in the Western World are based directly or indirectly upon his philosophy:

29D. TIM. Let us, then, state for what reason becoming and this universe were framed by him who framed them. He was good; and in the good no jealousy in any matter can ever arise. So, being without jealousy, he desired that all things should come as near as possible to being like himself. That this is the supremely valid principle of becoming and the order of the world, we shall most surely be right to accept from men

---

6. Ibid., pp. 54–55.

of understanding. Desiring, then, that all things should be good and, so far as might be, nothing imperfect, the god took over all that is visible—not at rest, but in discordant and unordered motion—and brought it from disorder into order, since he judged that order was in every way the better.[7]

47E. Now our foregoing discourse, save for a few matters, has set forth the works wrought by the craftsmanship of Reason; but we must now set beside them the things that come about of Necessity. For the generation of this universe was a mixed result of the combination of Necessity and Reason. Reason overruled Necessity by persuading her to guide the greatest part of the things that become towards what is best; in that way and on that principle this universe was fashioned in the beginning by the victory of reasonable persuasion over Necessity.[8]

In religions where this Artisan conception is held, the *Voice* ("He *spoke* and they were made; He *commanded,* and they were created." "God *said,* 'Let there be light, and there was light'.") and the *Hands* play an important role. The Voice symbolizes a life-giving Breath or Spirit, a Mind and an Intent. Wherever there is a Voice there is Intelligence; wherever there is a Breath there is Life; wherever there is Life there is a Spirit or Soul. (In one beautiful version of Genesis, God breathes on the face of the water.) The Hands go along with this. They symbolize the talented molding of the primeval clay or dust—a rational control and manipulation put into a product.

There are three possible renditions of this Artisan conception which can apply to God. The first is the traditional one and the accepted one:

(a) God can be thought of as an Artist who Creates a representation of an Idea already in His Mind. The order which Existence has is a copy of that completed Idea in His Mind.

If God has set this Idea going at a given Moment in Time and thereafter doesn't bother with it any more (except to perform miracles) then we can call that position *Deism.*

If God is at every moment operating upon the Material in the Universe and setting it going according to His

7. Francis M. Cornford, trans., *Plato's Cosmology* (New York: The Liberal Arts Press, 1957), p. 33. Used by permission of the Humanities Press, Inc., New York.

8. Ibid., p. 160.

completed Idea, then we can call that position *Theism*.

In general Deism holds to the complete separation of God and the Universe. God transcends the Universe and is different in His Nature from the Universe. He is no longer operating in the Universe. He has set up the Laws governing it according to His Idea. Occasionally He suspends the Laws of Nature and produces a beneficent event. This is called a miracle.

Theism believes that God is separate and different from the Universe, but He is intimately involved at any given moment in the course of affairs in man's history and the patternings of the Universe. God is an active, participating agent. He would be like the artist at the moments during which he is actually engaged in his creative process. God is thus Transcendent *and* Immanent.

(b) God could be thought of as an Artist who Creates from an initial idea in His Mind but which idea is only a kernel developed more fully and differently as time and the manipulation process go on. Writers, artists, composers talk about how creative thoughts and processes take hold and reveal themselves *during the act of creating,* and how different the end product is from the idea at inception. Sometimes the interrelationship of ideas and the structures of the materials lead the artist "uncontrollably" to his final product. It is as if the characters of the story, the sounds of the composition, the colors of the painting, take over, suggesting and forcing certain ways of expressing the creative act.

(c) God could be thought of as an Artist who creates without any initial idea at all to begin with, or with only a very minimal idea. Ideas to be followed through come during the act of engaging in an almost random, spontaneous manipulation of the material at hand. Picasso is said often times to have gone to his studio without any interest, without any ideas and just dabbed some color on a canvas. This set up possibilities to explore and the creative process began, but he didn't know where it would lead except for a few steps from the moment he was exploring the possibilities of what he then had on the canvas. (Of course we can argue that the end product was "potentially" in Picasso's mind. But what would "potentiality" then mean?

Nothing more than what did in fact come about as a final result. No matter what emerged as a final product we then could say it was "potentially" there.)

Depending on which of the three Artisan conceptions you wish to draw an analogy to, God will be conceived slightly differently. The last two suggest that God is more of an experimenter developing the possibilities to be followed through as these possibilities occur. None of the three necessarily imply a God who is in complete control, but One who is doing the best He can under the circumstances. The first *could* present a picture of an Omnipotent God in complete control, but then we have the Problem of Evil. Did He create Evil too? An Artisan conception of God who is not in complete control and has not Predetermined the Universe's existence right down to the last micro-second, at least has the virtue of being able to pass off the existence of Evil to things other than God such as "Necessity"; inherent evil or inherent obstructions in Matter; the existence of an opposing force in the Universe working against God's Goodness.

4.2 *The Creation of the Universe Ex Nihilo.* Most of the early Church Fathers accepted a fifth Creation concept against the reasonings of the Greek and Roman philosophers of the time. God Created the Universe not out of any pre-existing matter at all, not even out of a pre-existing Chaos, but "out of Nothing." The Universe—Matter—was *not* created or brought into what it is from anything which was in any way previously existing. The Church Fathers in adopting this position also went against much in the tradition of Hebrew thought. These early Church Fathers set forth a position that is still alive, although not universally accepted by all Christian thought. Christian proclamations such as the Fourth Lateran Council, the Syllabus of Pope Pius IX, and the Westminster Confession of Faith have affirmed God's Absolute *Creation Ex Nihilo.*

All the Church Fathers denied the eternality of Matter which was assumed in the Greek-Roman creation schemes. They all denied the Eternal coexistence of Matter qua Matter, with the Eternal God. Even in the Emanation theory which some Church Fathers accepted, "Matter" is in some incorporeal form present eternally in God's Being, but it begins its existence *as Matter* at a given moment in Time, which is determined by, and dependent upon, God's Creative Act of Unfolding. When that particular kind of Emanation takes place from God's Being, then it is Matter, but it is not in this material form eternally coexistent with God.

Here are a few of the many possible quotations from the Church Fathers illustrating the acceptance of God's Creating Ex Nihilo.[9]

Athanasius:

> . . . the world did not come into being of its own accord because it did not lack providence, and that neither was it made from pre-existent matter since God is not weak, but that through the Word God brought the universe, which previously in no way subsisted at all, into being from non-existence, as he says through Moses: *"In the beginning God made heaven and earth,"* and through the most helpful book of the Shepherd: *"First of all believe that God is one, who created and fashioned the universe and brought it from nonexistence into being."* This Paul too indicates when he says: *"By faith we understand that the worlds were formed by the word of God, so that the visible was not made from what is apparent."* For God is good—or rather the source of goodness—and the good has no envy for anything. Thus, because he envies nothing its existence, he made everything from nothing through his own Word, our Lord Jesus Christ.[10]

Theophilus:

> *God made* everything *out of what did not exist* (2 Macc. 7:28), bringing it into existence so that his greatness might be known and apprehended through his works.[11]

> Plato and his followers acknowledge that God is uncreated, the Father and Maker of the universe; next they assume that uncreated matter is also God, and say that matter was coeval with God (cf. Diels, Dox. 567, 13; 588, 17–18). But if God is uncreated and matter is uncreated, then according to the Platonists God is not the Maker of the universe, and as far as they are concerned the unique sovereignty of God is not demonstrated. Furthermore, as God is immutable because he is uncreated, if matter is uncreated it must also be immutable, and equal to God; for what is created is chargeable and mutable, while the uncreated is unchangeable and immutable.

---

9. Throughout I have used the Latin phrase Ex Nihilo for the sake of convenience and standardization. The Church Fathers writing in Greek used variations of such phrases as: ὁ δὲ κόσμος ἐξ οὐδενός or, ἐποίησε τα ὅτα οὐκ ὄντα πρότερον or, ἐκ τοῦ μὴ ὄντος εἰς τὸ εἶναι.

10. Robert W. Thomson, trans., *Athanasius: Contra Gentes and De Incarnatione* (London: Oxford University Press, 1971), p. 141. Copyright 1971 Oxford University Press and used by permission of The Clarendon Press, Oxford.

11. Grant, *Theophilus of Antioch ad Autolycum*, p. 7. Copyright 1970 Oxford University Press and used by permission of The Clarendon Press, Oxford.

What would be remarkable if God made the world out of pre-existent matter? Even a human artisan, when he obtains material from someone, makes whatever he wishes out of it. But the power of God is revealed by his making whatever he wishes out of the non-existent, just as the ability to give life and motion belongs to no one but God alone. For a man makes an image but cannot give reason or breath or sensation to what he makes, while God has this power greater than his: the ability to make a being that is rational, breathing, and capable of sensation. As in all these instances God is more powerful than man, so he is in his making and having made the existent out of the non-existent; he made whatever he wished in whatever way he wished.[12]

10. In the first place, in complete harmony they (The Prophets) taught us that he made everything out of the non-existent. For there was nothing coeval with God; he was his own locus; he lacked nothing; he *existed before the ages* (Ps. 54:20). He wished to make man so that he might be known by him; for him, then, he prepared the world. For he who is created has needs, but he who is uncreated lacks nothing.

Therefore God, having his own Logos innate in his own bowels (cf. Ps. 109:3), generated him together with his own Sophia, *vomiting him forth* (Ps. 44:2) before everything else. He used this Logos as his servant in the things created by him, and through him he made all things (cf. John 1:3). He is called Beginning because he leads and dominates everything fashioned through him. It was he, *Spirit of God* (Gen. 1:2) and *Beginning* (Gen. 1:1) and *Sophia* (Prov. 8:22) and *Power of the Most High* (Luke 1:35), who came down into the prophets and spoke through them about the creation of the world and all the rest (cf. 11.9).[13]

Tertullian:

. . . He can be known as God and be called the Almighty, save that He is no longer almighty, if His might did not extend to this also—to produce all things out of nothing! . . .

(Ch. 9) He cannot say that it was as its Lord that God made use of matter for the work of creating the world, for He could not be Lord of a substance which was coequal with Himself.[14]

---

12. Ibid., p. 27.

13. Ibid., pp. 39–41.

14. J. H. Wasznik, trans., *Tertullian: The Treatise Against Hermogenes* (London: Longmans. Green, 1956), p. 37. Used by permission of the publisher, Paulist/Newman Press.

. . . it remains that God undoubtedly made all things out of nothing . . . .

(Ch. 17) The fact of God being the One and only God asserts this rule, for He is the One-only God for the only reason that He is the sole God, and the sole God *for* the only reason that nothing existed with Him.[15]

For I say that, though Scripture did not clearly proclaim that all things were made out of nothing—just as it does not say either that they were made out of matter—there was not so great a need expressly to declare that all things had been made out of nothing as there would have been, if they had been made out of matter. 3. For in the case of that which is made out of nothing, it is clear that it was made out of nothing from the very fact that it is not shown to have been made out of something; nor is there any danger of its being thought to have been made out of something, when it is not indicated whence it was made. But in the case of that which is made out of something, unless the very fact that the thing in question was made out of something is clearly expressed by indication of whence it was made, there will be danger—first, that it appears to have been made out of nothing because its source is not mentioned; secondly, though it be of such a condition that it could not appear not to have been made out of something, there will be like danger of its appearing to have been made from a material far different from that out of which it was actually made, since its source is not indicated. 4. Therefore, if God could make all things out of nothing, Scripture could quite well omit to add that He had made them out of nothing, but it should have said by all means that He had made them out of matter, if He had done so; for the first possibility would be completely understandable, even if it was not expressly stated, but the second would be doubtful, unless it were stated.[16]

St. John of Damascus:

Now, because the good and transcendentally good God was not content to contemplate Himself, but by a super-abundance of goodness saw fit that there should be some things to benefit by and participate in His goodness, He brings all things from nothing into being and creates them, both visible and invisible, and man, who is made up of both. By thinking He creates, and, with the Word fulfilling and the Spirit perfecting, the object of His thought subsists.

---

15. Ibid., p. 48.

16. Ibid., pp. 55–56.

He is the maker and creator of the *angels.* He brought them from nothing into being and made them after His own image into a bodiless nature, some sort of spirit, as it were, and immaterial fire—as the divine David says: "Who maketh his angels spirits: and his ministers a burning fire." [17]

Our God, who is glorified in trinity and unity, Himself "made heaven and earth, and all things that are in them." He brought all things from nothing into being; some, such as heaven, earth, air, fire, and water, from no pre-existing matter; and others, such as animals, plants and seeds, He made from those things which had their existence directly from Him. For, by the Creator these last were made from earth, water, air and fire. [18]

The Ex Nihilo theory can be found in the other Church Fathers, in Augustine, in Aquinas, in Calvin, in Kierkegaard, and in others. Here is Aquinas' unique formulation:

I answer that, It is sufficiently apparent at first glance, according to what has preceded, that to create can be the proper action of God alone. For the more universal effects must be reduced to the more universal and prior causes. Now among all effects the most universal is being itself; and hence it must be the proper effect of the first and most universal cause, God. Hence we find it said that *neither intelligence nor the soul gives being, except inasmuch as it works by divine operation.* Now to produce being absolutely, and not merely as this or that being, belongs to the nature of creation. Hence it is manifest that creation is the proper act of God alone. [19]

Thus it appears that it is an act of much greater power to make a thing from nothing than from its contrary.

Reply Obj. 3. The power of the maker is reckoned not only from the substance of the thing made, but also from the mode of its being made; for a greater heat heats not only more, but also more quickly. Therefore, although to create a finite effect does not reveal an infinite power, yet to create it from nothing does reveal an infinite power. This appears from what has been said. For if a greater power is required in the agent in proportion to the distance of the potenti-

---

17. Frederic H. Chase, Jr., trans., *Saint John of Damascus Writings* (New York: Fathers of the Church, Inc., 1958), p. 205. Used by permission of the publisher, The Catholic University of America Press. Saint John (674–749) was the last of the Church Fathers.

18. Ibid., p. 210.

19. Anton C. Pegis, ed., *Introduction to St. Thomas Aquinas* (New York: The Modern Library, Random House, 1948), Q. 45, Art. 5, p. 243. Used by permission of the publisher.

ality from act, it follows that the power of that which produces
something from no presupposed potentiality (which is how a creating agent produces) is infinite, because there is no proportion between *no potentiality* and the potentiality presupposed by the power
of a natural agent, as there is no proportion between *non-being* and
being. And because no creature has an absolutely infinite power,
any more than it has an infinite being, as was proved above, it
follows that no creature can create.[20]

4.3 *The Presupposition of Creation Ex Nihilo By God.* There are
several presuppositions in the Creation Ex Nihilo belief which are shared
by those holding it:

(1) Matter, the Universe, is totally unlike God. Unlike God,
    Matter cannot be eternal.

(2) It is better and more superior to be eternal than not to
    be eternal. (In most ancient thought eternality and divinity
    were equated.)

(3) If Matter *were* Eternal like God, then Matter too would
    be divine. We would then have *two* Gods, or we would
    have something equal with God. (Remembering the on-
    tological argument, nothing whatever can be equal with
    God. There is, and can be, only One Supreme and Eternal
    God.) Therefore, matter must have been Created Ex Ni-
    hilo.

We can put this in another way—a way we shall be discussing in
detail in the next chapter:

(a) There was the persistent desire to present a God for belief
    who was utterly *independent,* self-sufficing, and self-con-
    tained from *All Existence,* and from *any* and *all* particular
    existences.

(b) All things were to be seen as completely and irrevocably
    dependent upon God for their presence and for their con-
    tinued existence. But God was to be seen as that Being
    who was not dependent in any way upon anything else
    for His Being or for His Source.

20. Ibid., p. 245.

(c) Matter is inherently limited and limiting. God is the Unlimited who by Limiting creates and necessitates the existence of Matter. God Creates the Necessary for the sake of a *Good*—namely Existence.

Thus Creation Ex Nihilo illustrates as nothing else can, the Unlimited and Unnecessitated Nature of God's Being.

The logic behind both these ways of presenting the motives implicit in the Creation Ex Nihilo belief is basically similar to the ontological argument: If God were Limited and Necessitated, then God would *not* be God for *that* other Unlimited and Unnecessitated Being would be God. If God were not the Unlimited and Unnecessitated Being then He would not be what He is—the Most Supreme and thus the highest object of religious devotion. Worship of anything less than this Most Supreme Being is idolatry. Worship of anything short of this is worship not of God, the Most Supreme of *All* but of a supreme object, or of objects. God is so Completely Perfect (and so Powerful) that He does not lack anything—not even the Power to bring into Being what was not in any way previously existing.

4.4 What Does "Create" Mean? To "create" means to make, produce, construct, shape. Men create houses, missiles, paintings. Creation implies the use of ideas, imagination, deliberation, and intention in an inventive way. It involves novelty—something new coming into existence that wasn't there before. It often involves uniqueness—something that can be differentiated as quite unlike other things around it. We often loosely apply the word to the reproductive process: humans "create" children, children are the "creation" of their parents. Sometimes we even use the word in such phrases as "creative accident" which occur in happenings, in mechanical or spontaneous paintings, and in chance occurrences. But in all such situations we are not assuming that something is being created out of nothing, or that something is coming from nothing. All such creations come out of matter previously existing in some form or other. There is some kind of rearrangement of pre-existing material by the use of power.

In the case of God's original Creation Ex Nihilo there is no pre-existing material to be worked upon. It is believed that God brings matter into existence from Total Nothingness. In the concept of Absolute Creation Ex Nihilo by God, we cannot legitimately assume that He created matter from a state which had the potentiality to produce matter. We would be contradicting the meaning of our concept if we did this. If Total

Nothingness were a state of potential, out of which God brought matter into existence, then Nothingness would not be Nothingness. It would be that State of potential for matter out of which God Created the Original Matter. It could not then be said that God created matter *out of Nothing.* He created matter from an already existing state which had the potential for matter. And this is not the meaning of Creation Ex Nihilo by God.[21]

The difference between God's creation of matter out of Nothing and ordinary creation is so vast that another word should be invented to apply to that kind of event or possibility. But here again we find the same linguistic and logical problems we had with reference to the meaning of a First Cause.[22] No other word would do any more justice to such a Creation Ex Nihilo Event or Possibility, simply because no such event can exist, and no such possibility is possible, since the concept is self-contradictory in meaning. It is not a matter of applying a new word but of constructing a noncontradictory meaning for the concept itself. Such a meaning cannot be constructed since there cannot logically without contradiction be an event with such a meaning.

Any ordinary linguistic meaning of creation implies pre-existing material to be worked, or pre-existing material that is in a process of change. No other meaning can be logically consistent. Creation Ex Nihilo cannot be a logically described event—whether it is done by God or is a natural process whereby something comes into existence out of Nothing. There would not be anything—no process of this kind—to be described. If there were, then it would not be that *Ex Nihilo* "event." There would never be any conditions known by which that something was coming (or did come) out of Nothing. There *are no conditions present to be known* at such an event. There could never be any knowledge of *when* or *how* this event was occurring or did occur.

4.5   *Can Something Come Out of Nothing?* The Greek philosophers such as Parmenides and his Eleatic School, as well as Plato and Aristotle, attempted to resolve conceptual problems with reference to the word

---

21. If the Creation by God Ex Nihilo belief falls back upon this qualified meaning of Total Nothingness as a State containing Matter potentially in some way, then the philosophical problem arises of describing logically what this potential could be like. If such a description can be presented, then you have a "something-or-other" not a "Nothingness." Thus it would be that "State of Potential" out of which Matter comes—or out of which God brings Matter—and *not* a *Nothing.*

22. Our point there was that such notions as an Absolute First Cause, First Beginning, First Moment, First Event, First Motion, are linguistically self-contradictory. The very meaning of words such as Cause, Beginning, Moment, Event, Motion imply a prior process to them, whereas the word *First* used in an Absolute sense has the meaning of denying such a prior process. The same kind of analysis will be applied here to the concept of Creation Ex Nihilo.

Nothing. There were many forms of negation in the Greek language. What concerned them was that the word for "Nothing"(such as οὐδέν, μηδέν) was a noun. Nouns for them were substantive—they referred to persons, places, and things. We have the same semantical and syntactical variations in our language: "Nothing is there." "I did Nothing." "Nothing bothers me." "Nothing exists." "First there was Nothing, and then there was something." [23]

For the Greeks and Romans the paradox of Nothing was this: If "Nothing" is a noun, and if a noun stands as the name for something, then "Nothing" must *mean* that *something* and it therefore can't mean Nothing which is what you want it to mean. Now if "Nothing" isn't a noun and hence does not refer to anything at all, then why do we use it in our language as a noun, and how is it possible to talk about it—Nothing—if it isn't anything at all to be talked about? This kind of philosophizing laid the foundations for the distinction between a grammatical noun and a semantical noun. Nouns need not refer only to substantive things such as persons, places, and things. Some nouns, especially in philosophy, can be used to refer to processes, functions, and activities—in this case the process of wanting to negate or deny.

All the Greek and Roman philosophies assumed a common perspective about Nothing:

> (1) Absolute Nothing cannot have any existence whatever. There was never a time at which there was absolutely Nothing. There was always a time at which something was in existence. Existence is Eternal. There was always something in existence in an Eternal Time.

We can quote two passages about Melissus, a disciple of Parmenides, to illustrate this first perspective. The first quotation is from Aristotle and the other two are from Simplicius:

> 7.19 Melissus says that if anything is, it is eternal, since it is impossible for anything to come into being out of nothing. For whether all things have come to be, or not all, in either case they are eternal. For if they came into being, they would have to come

---

23. It might be worthwhile to think about these two passages before continuing:

"I see nobody on the road," said Alice. "I only wish I had such eyes," the King remarked in a fretful tone. "To be able to see Nobody. And at that distance too! Why it's as much as I can do to see real people, by this light!"—*Alice Through the Looking Glass.*

"The Not does not come into being through negation, but negation is based on the Not, which derives from the nihilation of Nothing."—Heidegger.

to be out of nothing. For if all things have come into existence, then nothing existed previously. If (on the other hand) some things (already) existed, and others were continually added to them, then what is would have become more and greater; and if it did grow more and greater, the addition would come into being out of nothing.

7.20 What was always was and always will be. For if it had come into being, it necessarily follows that before it came into being nothing was. But if nothing was, nothing could in any way come to be out of nothing.

7.21 Since, therefore, it did not come into being, it is and always was and always will be, and has no beginning or end, but is infinite. For if it had come into being, it would have a beginning (for it would have begun to come into being at some time) and an end (for it would have ceased to come into being at some time). But since it neither began nor ceased, it is and was and always will be, and has neither beginning nor end.[24]

(a) The Greek and Roman Atomists did believe in the existence of a Void or empty space existing between atoms in which space the atoms swirled and moved. But this Void did not create anything nor could something be created with it, or out of it.

(b) There was also the belief among Greek and Roman philosophers that the Universe was Finite and beyond that there was Nothing at All. This Nothingness too was devoid of any powers or potentialities, since it was no existence in any way.

(2) *Nothing can come from "Nothing."* Something cannot be created out of Nothing. As Lucretius put it: *Creatio ex nihilo nihil fit.* Something cannot come from Nothing. Phrases such as these applied to both Absolute Nothing and to the Void. Something can only come from Something. Something can only be created from pre-existing material. If something did come from, or came out of, Nothing, then that Nothing would not be Nothing, but would be that Something from which, or out of which, the something came.

---

24. From *An Introduction to Early Greek Philosophy*, by John Mansley Robinson. Houghton Mifflin Company, 1968, pp. 140–42. Reprinted by permission of the publishers.

(3) Nothing cannot bring forth anything. If it did, or could, it then would not be Nothing but that power, or something, which has brought forth what it has brought forth.

For the Greek and Roman philosophers, Nothing is causally inefficacious. Our language, as theirs did, forces us for the sake of simplicity and convenience to speak loosely as if a Nothing is causally efficiacious. "The *lack* of Vitamin C causes scurvy." "Black is *produced* by the *absence* of color." But it is not the "lack of" that causes scurvy. "Lack of," "the absence of," cannot cause anything since it isn't anything to be able to cause something. Scurvy is caused by the complex existing biochemical reactions which take place in the body. Add vitamin C, and all things being equal another reaction is obtained.

This philosophical position did not prevent the Greeks and Romans from asserting that indeed new things can come, and do come, into existence which were not in existence in any similar way before. But this does not mean that they come from Nothing. It merely means the coming-into-existence of something (from something previously existing) that is novel, unique, and different from anything previously existing. And they come into existence by means of an eternal retransformation of the infinite possibilities of an infinite eternally existing Universe. From one point of view everything that exists can be seen to be novel, unique, and different. (The Principle of Difference in Identity.) From another point of view everything that exists can be seen to be to some degree similar to everything else that exists. (The Principle of Identity in Difference.) Variety and Identity can be found in everything that exists. But they come from things previously existing.

4.6 Can God Himself Create Ex Nihilo? Granted, it is true that *"Something cannot come from Nothing."* But maybe this is true only in *our* logic. Perhaps there is another kind of logic or reality where this would not be true and where "Something can come into existence from Nothing." Perhaps there is some Power great enough to bring this about, although we might never be able to know it since it doesn't fit into our logic and will always remain a mystery.

Let's discuss these points with reference to the God concept.

(1) "We can't Create Out of Nothing in *our* logic. But God can Create out of Nothing in *His* Logic. Our logic is finite and His is Infinite."

Creation ex nihilo falls into the same category as "square-circle," "circular-square,' "four-sided triangles," "a thing is wholly both at *A* and not *A* at the same time." These are definitional self-contradictions and are impossible in *any* logic provided that the meanings of the individual words are retained. Assuming that there are multi-logics, if we presented any other logic with the meaning of a square, and the meaning of a circle, then it would *still* be impossible meaningfully to construct a notion of a "square-circle" or a "circular-square." No matter how hard we tried, or what logic we used, if the same meanings for square and circle are kept then such notions would remain self-contradictory in *any* logic—even God's. God cannot overcome the contradictory nature of "square-circle" even in His Logic regardless of how "Infinite" His Logic may be.

It is not a problem of our not knowing *what* God's Logic is *like*. It is a matter of meanings with which a logic, *any* logic, must deal. In so far as these meanings for "square" and for "circular" are carried over into God's Logic, then God's Logic cannot make them consistent no matter what the logical form into which they are fitted. We could change the meanings of "square" and "circular" when we take them into another logic or into God's Logic, in order to make them consistent and not self-contradictory, but then we would not be dealing with a square or a circle. Whatever we did have would not be the attempt to get a "square-circle" but something else.

This same analysis can be applied to the notion of *Creation Ex Nihilo*. Since it is a contradiction in terms then it would be a logical impossibility even in God's Logic or any reality. Self-contradictions have no existence in reality. Self-contradictions can only appear in the realm of language or definitions which is the only possible place for them since they are meanings that *exclude* any possibility of their being the case in external reality.[25]

(2) "*We* can't Create Ex Nihilo because we haven't enough Power. If we had enough Power, we could do it. God being *Omnipotent* is Powerful enough to *Create Ex Nihilo*."

---

25. Languages have interesting features. (1) They can be used to deceive. (A language is truly a language if we can lie with it.) (2) They can present concepts such as The Infinite which cannot be imaged, but only definitionally conceptualized. (3) They can present nonconceptualizable notions such as "square-circles." (4) They can present notions which do not refer to anything in particular such as "God is Limitless," "God is Pure Spirit," "The cause of the poem was within himself," "You have the ability, if only you would make the effort." (5) They contain words which refer to everything or anything at all, and thus to nothing in particular such as "thing," "exists," "whole," "part of." (6) They contain words which, once given a meaning, cannot in any sense ever be allowed *in application* to mean that which they were invented to mean such as Nothing, God, The Infinite.

Power—*no matter how much*—has nothing to do with being able to bring into existence self-contradictions such as square-circles and Creation Ex Nihilo. Ordinary creation involves power. The coming-into-existence of something from some previous existence involves power. But Creation—the bringing-into-existence, or the coming-into-existence of something from a Nothing—can never be related to power. All the power one could wish would not be able to make a thing "both *be* and *not be* at the same time and in the same respect." All the Power a God could ever have would not be able to bring something (matter) into existence out of Nothing.

No models or analogies at all are possible with reference to God's *Power to Create Ex Nihilo*, nor are they possible with reference to "*Something coming from Nothing.*" It is not that no adequate model from human experience can ever be drawn to unique situations such as these (including First Cause, First Event, First Motion) but that there isn't anything there in any way *in* the first place to which any analogy *can* be drawn since these meanings in their contradictory nature like square-circles *exclude* all possible realities and experiences of them.

This is not saying that we cannot draw analogies with reference to *God's Power*. We cannot draw analogies to God's *Power to create out of Nothing*. God is said to be *Omnipotent*. This may mean that God is All-Powerful in the sense that He can do *anything at all*. This interpretation of Omnipotence runs head-on into problems. If God can do anything at all, can He do the impossible? Can He construct a square-circle? Can He change the past? Can He form a rock big enough that He can't move? Can He lie? Can He kill Himself and never come back to life again?

Omnipotence must be defined in terms of possibilities. Not even God can perform impossibilities since they are not things that can exist or can be done. Omnipotence then would have to be defined in some way as: "God is All-Powerful. He has the power to do anything that is possible (if He wants to, or feels it is worthwhile doing). Everything is possible with God, except the impossible." Since Creation Ex Nihilo is an impossibility God cannot create Matter out of Nothing.

The appeal to mystery or to faith will not do. Creation by God Ex Nihilo cannot be regarded as a mystery which the human mind cannot in any way comprehend or conceptualize. The extent to which the meaning of the phrase *Creation Ex Nihilo* is understood to that extent it is not a mystery. The moment Creation Ex Nihilo is seen as contradictory, then it can be seen to be an impossible state of affairs about which no mystery can be involved since there is no state of affairs possible to have any mystery about.

The same applies to the attitude of faith. We may have faith in something, about something, even faith *in spite of* evidence for something, but if there is nothing existing in the first place to have faith about then the act of faith is not only ungrounded but completely misplaced and without content. Faith of itself does not provide supporting evidence for anything. It does provide such things as psychological reassurances and attitudes to be taken toward things. It may even provide a dogged insistence on the correctness of an idea. It may provide perspectives from which to relate to events and people. But faith that Creation Ex Nihilo does take place cannot be had. There is nothing there in the first place to have faith in. If the attitude of faith is a supporting ground for the validity of an idea, then by the same token one can by faith give supporting ground to any notion whatever. By an act of faith God could be said *not* to Create Ex Nihilo, but He is Co-Eternal with the Universe. By an act of faith it could be said that God does not exist, or that *many* Gods exist, or that God isn't here yet, or that God passed out of existence years ago. Unguarded, both the appeal to mystery and the appeal to faith tend to become arguments from ignorance or arguments to ease the burden of something unknown or unacceptable.

4.7 "When" Did God Create? In the Creation Ex Nihilo of Matter by God theories, this original Matter was created *instantaneously*—at an *instant in time*. Geneological studies of the Bible have been done by many scholars including Bishop Usher and the seventeenth-century Cambridge Hebrew scholar Dr. John Lightfoot, which have placed the Creation by God on October 23rd, 4004 B.C. at nine o'clock in the morning. God took six days to separate, shape, and adorn His Creation. On the seventh day He rested. Each day may be taken symbolically to mean millions, or billions, or trillions of years. This brings up the matter of how long is the seventh day, and are we now in the seventh day period with God still resting? Will there be a new Monday, or First Day again, which the belief "Coming of the Lord" might signify? Will God totally annihilate the Universe when He gets up from His rest and create a new Universe—or will He re-create out of the old existing Matter?

We can answer the question *"When did God Create the Universe Ex Nihilo"* by answering that *God created the Universe at a time when there was no Time.* God created Time along with the Universe. There was *No Time* before that First Instantaneous Creation Moment—only God. It was God minus the Universe.

We get into some interesting puzzles with this belief. What was God doing (in His Time) for an eternity into His past before He Created the Universe Ex Nihilo? God existed by Himself through an Eternity before the Creation without needing a Universe. Why did He suddenly desire to create the Universe?

If the Sufficient Reason for the Universe is God, and if this Sufficient Reason God is Eternal, must not the Universe itself in some way be Eternal also? If this is not the case, then there must have been a Time when God, the Sufficient Reason, existed but the thing it was the Sufficient Reason for did not exist. And if it did *not* exist, then God the Sufficient Reason for it could not exist, since we need God as the Sufficient Reason for its existence.

The sufficient reason for the existence of something cannot exist without the existence of that thing for which it is the sufficient reason. A thing exists only in so far as its sufficient reason for existing exists, otherwise it can have no existence. It is difficult, if not impossible, to hold that God existed eternally not being the sufficient reason *until* He created *Ex Nihilo* at which time He *then* became the sufficient reason.

We could say that God was Timeless—not Temporal at all, not Everlasting or Eternal. Time just does not at all apply to him before His Creation of Time along with the Universe. This approach presents these problems: If Time does not apply to God, if God is Timeless, then such a Being cannot have a history since history is temporal. To say that this Timeless God *began Time along with the Universe at a time when there was no Time* implies that at that moment when He initiated this Unique Event He was engaged *in* a Time, or *at* a Time in order to bring this Event about. He did something. What brought *that* Event about? In attempting to answer this we construct a history and a time-sequence thereby making God's activity a temporal and not a timeless act. God as an Active Being cannot be Timeless.

It is impossible to talk about a *Being*—even God—that *exists* at Zero-time, or No-Time. At what time was that No-Time or Zero-Time? Phrases such as: "I was *born* at Zero-Time, or No-Time" (this is *not* the same as saying that "I was *not* born"), "when I *was* Zero-years old," are contradictory. Every time, like every event, is conditioned by a previous time. We cannot intelligibly ask "At what time did Time begin?" We cannot without self-contradiction think of a time which has no preceding time to it anymore than we can think of a present without a past. The notion of *Time began at a time when there was No-Time* contradicts itself because it says that Time began at a time when there was *No Time* for it to begin at—or at which it could begin.

Kant in the second part of his First Antimony (we presented a discussion of the first part in 3.8) describes it this way:

The world has no beginning and no limits in space, but is infinite, in respect both to time and space.

PROOF

For let us assume that it has a beginning. Then, as beginning is an existence which is preceded by a time in which the thing is not, it would follow that antecedently there was a time in which the world was not, that is, an empty time. In an empty time, however, it is impossible that anything should take its beginning, because of such a time no part possesses any condition as to existence rather than non-existence, which condition could distinguish that part from any other (whether produced by itself or through another cause). Hence, though many a series of things may take its beginning in the world, the world itself can have no beginning, and in reference to time past is infinite.[26]

If the Universe is said to have Begun at T, then it might equally have Begun at T^1. And if the Universe can be said to have begun at T^1 then it could very well have Begun at T^2. This could be carried on ad infinitum. No part of an empty Time can ever be picked out as providing a sufficient condition for the world to start. No part of a Time without events occurring can ever serve as the distinguishing condition for a First Beginning. It would thus be a contradiction to say that the Universe had a First Beginning *in* Empty Time, or *at* a Time when there was No-Time. This would be admitting the contradictory state of affairs that the Universe began *at a Time* when there was No-Time at which it could begin.

A First Beginning could never occur since for it to occur *in Time* is to occur *at a Time* in a series of events. If it occurred in an Empty Time (No-Time) there could be no such series of events since an event implies a time. There is thus an infinite extension of beginnings, or events, and an infinite extension of Time.

We could put this in another way: There can be *no* Time at which a First Creation, or First Beginning could ever occur, since for it to occur in Time, is to occur at a Time, and for it to occur at a Time is to occur in a Time. This implies an infinite extension of Time and hence an infinite extension of Beginnings (activity).

26. Theodore Meyer Greene, ed., *Kant Selections* (New York: Charles Scribner's Sons, 1929), p. 191. Used by permission of the publisher.

But can there not be a Time when, or at which, there was mere Nothingness—Wholly Empty Space? ("Wholly Empty Space" is a contradiction in terms since it cannot have location or any dimension which is the very meaning of the word "Space.") This would be saying that time existed and time was passing without absolutely anything at all occurring. But how can "time exist or pass" without anything at all occurring since this is the way in which we know that time has passed—by things occurring. Time is a measure of change. This would be similar to having "Space" without anything in Existence at all, or trying to define "space" without reference to any thing in particular in existence. The essential problem is not that of not being able to tell how much time has passed in that "Wholly Empty Space" or that "Total Nothingness," but there cannot be any passing of time at all any more than there can be a triangle without lines, or an airplane flying without leaving the ground.

The Universe does not come from Nothingness either on its own or by God's Power. If the Universe did come from Nothingness, there would be no previous time and no previous space for it to come from. If we ask "Where did the Universe come from?", our answer can only be: "It doesn't come from anywhere." (This is not the same as saying that it comes from Nothing.) It doesn't have to come from anywhere because the Universe exists eternally in some form or another. In fact, there isn't any "where" from which it could come. There cannot be any previous place or space for it to be in because it is "All that there is" and includes all places and spaces. Every particular thing in the Universe comes from somewhere and from some place, but not the Universe itself.

4.8 Why Do Things Exist Rather Than "Nothingness"? There are two allied questions that seem to perplex people:

(1) Why do (should) things exist rather than there being Nothing? Why is there a Universe rather than there being Nothingness?

(2) Why do (should) things exist the way they do rather than some other way? Why aren't things *different* from what they are? (We shall discuss this question in more detail in the succeeding few chapters especially with reference to the Principle of Sufficient Reason in chapter 6.)

The first, perhaps more than the second, question stems from an awe and wonder and fascination at there being anything at all in existence. The question though is illformed. The choice is not, and can never be, between the existence of the Universe and the "existence" of Nothingness. Something or other, the Universe, has had to be in Existence in some way or another without there ever being a time when there was no Existence, or no Universe. The very act of awe, wonderment, and fascination is itself based upon, and is a response to, the existence of the Universe.

4.9 "Why" Did God "Create"? There have been many answers to this question. It would seem that you could construct as many answers as you cared to, limited only by the framework of the kind of God which is accepted. It will have to be assumed that there is a God, and that that God *did* Create the Universe. Here is a small list of some of the answers which have been given in the history of thought:

(1) Because of God's over-abundant Goodness, He could not help but Create the Universe. Existence is a Good. To exist is a good. Existence is better than nonexistence. Existence is the source of all possible goods, of all possible values such as Truth, Beauty, Perfection which are also Good. Existence is the overflow of God's Goodness.

(2) God, being for an Eternity unto-Himself and by Himself, wanted something upon which He could bestow His Perfect and Unending Love. Man being the highest of the creations in Existence, and the Crowning Glory, is that upon which God principally wishes to bestow His Love. The most perfect evidence of this is God's sacrifice in an act of Love, of His only begotten Son, Jesus Christ. Man of course may not feel this Love and may not want to respond to it. To the extent that this is so, to that extent man is bereft of true love and alienated from his True Source.

(3) God, being for an Eternity unto-Himself and by Himself, wished for something to love Him and to glorify Him. God Created the Universe for the purpose of being loved by man who can recognize Him as the Supreme Being. All institutions, all human activities, should be dedicated in some measure to the fulfillment of this love and honor for God. (The Mass, for example, is not performed primarily in order to educate people, or to keep them true to the faith or to provide an aesthetic and spiritual enhancement of human life. The Mass is firstly performed

for the glory and glorification of God. Whether there are humans around or not it is the duty of the Priest to present Mass regularly for the sake of expressing a love for God, though of course in the process the Priest's own life is enhanced with love and humility, as are the witnesses to the Mass.)

(4) God Created the Universe in order to arrive at Man. God could have Created the Universe without man. But He wanted to Create something which had His Image. In Creating man in His Image, man must see by means of that image, that he was Created with a special Purpose which he must strive to achieve. That Purpose must be understood in the light of God's Creation toward an Ultimate Goal. Man was Created with potentialities. Man's purpose is related to God's Love. God has provided gifts for man to develop his potentialities to the utmost in accordance with God's Intentions.

(5) God Created Man along with the Universe to have Man as a copartner in achieving God's Plan. God's Plan will not be achieved—and God does not want it to be achieved without the assistance of Man in his growing and developing into a God-like creature. Whether man will become God-like, good, loving, compassionate, or not is an open question which God has left up to man's free will to decide. It is up to man to organize himself and make the decision.

V

God as the Necessary Being: The Sustaining Cause for Existence

5.1 Introduction. We have examined the horizontal or serial feature of Aquinas' first two Ways. Now we have to discuss the vertical, or underlying ground, or "ontological cause" feature of the arguments. This vertical feature purportedly operates even if there is an infinite regress—even if the horizontal series is Infinite. We arrive at that Being which maintains, preserves and necessitates the order found in that infinite series. We shall present this vertical dimension in the context of Aquinas' Third Way.

The Third Way of Aquinas is the argument from Possibility and Necessity. It is sometimes referred to specifically as the Argument from Contingency. (Aquinas did not use the word "contingent.") All the Five Ways—and indeed in some way or another all arguments for God's existence—presuppose a Necessary Being upon which all things depend for their being, but which Necessary Being depends on nothing else for Its own Being. All the Five Ways take the Universe to be an *effect* of this Necessary Being. This Necessary Being is a Cause of order, motion, efficient causation, values, and of Existence itself. All the Five Ways presuppose a Necessary Being who acts upon the Universe, who creates it, supports it, maintains it, moves it, and is its Operating Intelligence and Source of Values. Each of the arguments in its own manner tries to show how a finite, limited, conditioned, contingent Universe is derived from some Infinite, Unlimited, Unconditioned, Necessary, and Eternal

Source which is completely different in essential respects from its product. We shall examine in this chapter whether or not it is correct to say that things which exist in the Universe cannot exist at any given time *as they are unless* there is something else which is quite different from them which also exists at that time as their Sustaining Cause. Aquinas is right in saying that everything in the Universe which exists depends upon something other than itself in order to exist as that thing, or in that way. But from this truth to saying that for things to be what they are in the Universe depends upon something other than their relatedness to each other, such as a Sustaining Being, is a further step which is difficult to support.

The first two Ways clearly show for Aquinas what he develops in more detail in the Third Way: that *existence depends upon something other than itself.* Existence is contingent. Things of themselves cannot account for their own existence. All a posteriori arguments for God's existence discuss the existence of *specific* finite things (motion, causes, order, disorder, perfection, goodness, beauty in things) and then proceed to relate these specific finite things to God who is their Source. The Third Way argues generally from the existence of finite things—any and all finite things—to the existence of a Necessary Being as their Source. The Third Way argues from finite things as being contingent to the necessity of a Noncontingent or Necessary Being which we call God. From the a posteriori knowledge that it is possible for things to begin to exist at some time and possible for them to cease to exist at some time, Aquinas concludes that there must exist a Necessary Being, such that it is impossible for It to begin to exist at some time, and impossible for It to cease to exist at any time. He—God—exists Necessarily.

5.2 *The Third Way: The Argument.*

The third way is taken from possibility and necessity, and runs thus. We find in nature things that are possible to be and not to be, since they are found to be generated, and to be corrupted, and consequently, it is possible for them to be and not to be. But it is impossible for these always to exist, for that which can not-be at some time is not. Therefore, if everything can not-be, then at one time there was nothing in existence. Now if this were true, even now there would be nothing in existence, because that which does not exist begins to exist only through something already existing. Therefore, if at one time nothing was in existence, it would have been impossible for anything to have begun to exist; and thus even now nothing would be in existence—which is absurd. Therefore, not all beings are merely possible, but there must exist something the existence of which is necessary. But every necessary thing either has its necessity caused by another, or not. Now it is impossible to go on to infinity in necessary things which have their necessity caused by another, as has been already proved in regard to efficient causes. Therefore we cannot but admit the existence of some being having of itself its own necessity, and not receiving it from another, but rather causing in others their necessity. This all men speak of as God.[1]

That there are "contingent" things is an a posteriori truth for Aquinas. If he means by this that our experience shows that things depend upon other things for their existence, then he is correct. If he means that our experience shows us that things exist and then don't exist, then he is again correct. But if Aquinas means that our experience shows us that "it is possible that all things begin to exist and that *all* things *cease* to exist," then he is not correct for our experience does not show us this. It might even be argued that no (a posteriori) experience can ever be had of what is "possible" or "not possible" in time. It may be the case that everything that exists is "possible to be" at one time and "not to be" at another time.

It also might be the case that it would be "impossible for these always to exist" (impossible for them to be eternal) since by definition "that which is possible not to be at some time, *is not* (in existence sometime)." But though these may be true statements it does not follow that "then at one time there could have been nothing (at all) in existence." It could be the case that there are always things in existence that were not in existence before, which things give rise to other existences that were not in existence before, and which come from other existences that were not in existence before . . . the process going on ad infinitum and eternally. There never was a time at which there was Nothing in existence, but all that *was* in existence, and *is* in existence at some time, will no longer be in existence in that way again.

There may be a time at which any particular thing can be seen not to exist, but from this we cannot jump to the conclusion that there would be a time at which *Nothing at all* would exist. There could be an infinite series of contingent events each of them finite, so that no moment ever occurs which does not have some of these contingent events happening. Different things could exist at different times but yet at any given time there would always be some things existing. Things may constantly be in a process of coming-into-being at the same time that things are passing-out-of-being. Clearly you cannot go from the statement, *For every particular existing thing, there is a time when it is not in existence,* to *Therefore, there is a time when Everything is not in existence.*

---

1. Anton C. Pegis, ed., *Introduction to St. Thomas Aquinas* (New York: Random House, 1967), *Summa Theologica*, Q. 2, Art. 3, pp. 24–27. Used by permission of the publisher.

It is impossible that contingent things always exist. But this is not the same as saying that there is, or can be, a time at which all contingent things do not exist—or at which all at the *same time* exemplify their "possibility" *not to exist.* Even if every thing in the Universe *is* contingent still there need not be some time in the past when *Nothing* existed.

This is a Universe in which every thing in it is contingent—every thing in it can be "found to be generated, and to corrupt," every thing in it can be seen to change and to lose the existence it had before, and every thing in it which exists now will at some time cease to exist as it is now. None of this means that it loses its *total* existence. None of this means that existence can become totally Nothing.

5.3   The Assumptions in the Third Way. Aquinas' argument is a *reductio ad absurdum* similar in pattern to the denial of an Infinite Regress of beginnings which we examined in 3.8. There Aquinas and Kant argued that the Infinite regress couldn't come into a Now. Similarly in *this* argument an Infinite Regress would have come to a Nothing-Point sometime in its career and "thus even now nothing would be in existence."

If every thing in the Universe is "contingent," there must not be an infinite time span, or series of contingent events into the past. There must be at least one thing that is Noncontingent, or Necessary, which exists throughout all change and is not dependent upon anything else for anything, not even Its Existence, and which never ceases to exist but is always, was always, and will always be what it is in Itself.

If these contingent things occurred in an Infinite Time span into the past, then there would not be any present moment. At the present moment there would be *Nothing* at all. Why? Because since everything is contingent given an Infinite amount of time then at *some* time in that Past Infinite Time Span *Everything* that is contingent will not exist. If everything were contingent (*possible not to be*) then there would have been a time when *Nothing* at all existed, and nothing would Now exist, which is absurd since things *do* Now exist. If there was a time when Nothing existed, then nothing at all could ever have come to exist except with the aid of God, The Necessary Being, since there would be *Nothing*, no Cause, no Creator to bring things into Existence. Since things *do* exist, and since things *are* contingent, there must be something which is *not* contingent which is their Cause and this we call God.

Aquinas is assuming: (1) that this Nothing-Point would have already been reached in the Infinite Time Stream. (Aquinas ignored the possibility that perhaps such a Nothing-Point is yet to come.) And (2) that *Everything* at some time *ceases to be at the same time* in this Infinite Past Time Span. But because things cease to be what they were does not mean that they cease to be in any way at all—or become Nothing. When Aquinas for the sake of argument assumes an Infinite Past Time, he then must also assume the existence of an infinite number of contingent events or existent objects. If a contingent event is one that depends on something *other than itself* for its existence, then on the assumption of an Infinite Time there would have to be an Infinite number of contingent events. If you define "contingent" as depending upon something else other than another contingent event, a Necessary Being, then we are already assuming what has to be shown to be the case as well as equivocating on the meaning of "contingent."

Aquinas omitted the reference to a Time when there was Nothing when he presented a version of this argument in his *Summa Contra Gentiles*, Bk. II, chap. 15, sec. 6. But even if we remove this Nothing-Point notion in the argument and admit the existence of an Infinite Time and an Infinite Series of contingent events happening in that Time, stressing only the connection between a contingent Universe of Infinite duration and a Noncontingent Being or Ground for that Universe, we still get into other insurmountable problems.

5.4 Is It Possible That Every Thing That Exists in the Infinite Series Exists Only Contingently Without a Sustaining Cause or Necessary Being?

If the Universe is regarded as an infinite temporal series of motions, causes, and contingent events, then it needs no explanation in terms of a First Originator of the Series. It would be unintelligible to assert that God is the First Cause of *this* particular Infinite Series rather than another Infinite Series which could have taken place. It would be unintelligible to assert that God "chooses" *this* particular Infinite Series rather than another one. If the Series is an All-inclusive *Infinite Series* then there is no other one to compare it to and say that there is *another Infinite Series* which would be possible to choose from rather than the present Infinite Series. Not even God could choose another All-Inclusive Infinite Series over this one if there are no others to be chosen. God would be dealing *with*, or *in*, an *Infinite Series* and sustaining the process of a particular ongoing Infinite Series. He would not be choosing one out of a number of Infinite Series.

None of this denies that it is possible for there to have been *another* ordered Infinite Series in existence rather than this present one. The Universe can without inconsistency be viewed as a collection of occurrences whose series could have been otherwise than it is. There could have been an entirely different series of collections of occurrences having totally different causal connections and patterns of movements thereby having an entirely different order of events. There could be an infinite number of variations of the order of this Infinite Series that could have taken place. The existence of the order that actually did take place prevents any others from taking place—as yet. If the Series is an All-Inclusive Infinite Series, then anything in it which is physically possible to be would be. In this Infinite Series, whatever could come about would come about at the time it did come about without the necessity of a Necessary Being or Sustaining Cause. Given enough Time—and there would be enough time in an Infinite Time—even that which a Sustainer is assumed to do would be done.

Does this imply the possibility then that at some time in the Infinite Series there will appear a Necessary Being, or a Sustaining Cause? This would depend on whether or not the notion of a Necessary Being is a self-contradiction. If it is a self-contradiction then it cannot be a physical possibility. If it is not a self-contradiction it would then be incompatible with the concept of an All-Inclusive Infinite Series that takes care of itself, that is, is Eternally contingent and only contingent.

On the assumption that the All-Inclusive Infinite Series does take care of itself, it is possible to view everything that exists as existing only contingently. This view would involve concepts such as:

(1) Any thing that presently exists in the Universe need not have come about nor need it have come about at this time rather than another. If the set of conditions prior to any Now had been different, then the Now would have been different and that particular event would not have been as it is. Or something else would have existed instead.

(2) Any thing that exists at any particular time can be viewed as at some other time not to be what it *was.*

(3) Any particular thing is a process which is dependent upon other things being in a process for its existence and cannot become this thing of itself. Every particular thing points to something other than itself for its process but does not point to something *outside* the interrelated contingent series such as a Necessary Being or a Sustaining Cause for the process. In this sense the Universe is "self-explanatory." The Universe is an Infinite Collection of contingent events. All occurrences which produce contingent events are themselves contingent ad infinitum without there being any Necessary occurrences in the Universe, and without there being any Necessary Being in the Universe.

On the assumption that the Infinite Series *cannot* take care of itself, and that there is a God, it is intelligible to ask, "What keeps this Infinite Series going the particular way it does, rather than another way?" God would be the Sustaining Cause, not the *First Cause,* of things in this Infinite Series at any and every given moment. God would be that Necessary Being who makes the order in the Infinite Series be what it is rather than its being some other order. This would be a God who does not choose *That* the Universe should be, but chooses *What* it will be. He is not the "Creator" but the "Preserver." For the Infinite Series to be fully explained there must be a reference to a Necessary Being or Sustaining Cause which is Infinite and Co-Eternal with the Universe.

Is there such a Sustaining Cause? Do we have an inadequate and incomplete explanation of the Universe and the Infinite Series unless we refer to this Necessary Being? Is the Universe rendered unintelligible without postulating the existence of God?

VI

God as the Necessary Being: The Sufficient Reason for Existence

6.1 The Principle of Sufficient Reason and the Principle of Causality. What goes by the name of the "Principle of Sufficient Reason" has been in some way presupposed by philosophers such as Plato, Aristotle, Augustine, Aquinas, Leibniz, Kant, and many others down to the present time. We shall quote extensively from Leibniz to illustrate the principle, because his elaboration is a good one and also because it is the one most commonly referred to. One cannot help seeing the stark similarities with Aquinas' arguments with which we have already dealt.

> 32. . . . the principal of *sufficient reason*, by virtue of which we hold that no fact can be true or existing and no statement truthful without a sufficient reason for its being so and not different; albeit these reasons most frequently must remain unknown to us. . . .

> 36. A *sufficient reason*, however, must also exist for *contingent truths* or *truths of fact*, that is, for the series of things comprehended in the universe of creatures. Here the resolution into particular reasons could be continued without limit; for the variety of natural things is immense, and bodies are infinitely divided. There is an infinity of figures and movements, past and present, which contribute to the efficient cause of my presently writing this. And there is an infinity of minute inclinations and dispositions of my soul, which contribute to the final cause of my writing.

37. Now, all of this detail implies previous or more particular contingents, each of which again stands in need of a similar analysis to be accounted for, so that nothing is gained by such an analysis. The sufficient or ultimate reason must therefore exist outside the succession or series of contingent particulars, infinite though this series may be.

38. Consequently, the ultimate reason of all things must subsist in a necessary substance, in which all particular changes may exist only virtually as in its source: this substance is what we call *God.*

39. Now, this substance is the sufficient reason for all this particular existence which is, moreover, interconnected throughout. Hence, there is but one God, and this God suffices.

40. This Supreme Substance is unique, universal, and necessary. There is nothing existing apart from it which would be independent of it, and the existence of this being is a simple consequence of its possibility. It follows that this substance does not admit of any limitation and must contain as much reality as is possible.[1]

For Leibniz the Universe is an aggregate of finite things and events. No Sufficient Reason for it can be found either in any particular finite thing in the Universe or in the whole aggregate of things. God is a "Dominant Unity" who rules the Universe and who constructs it, who is Supranatural, and who is the "Ultimate Reason" for why things happen as they do rather than another way. God provides us with the Reason for the Universe and for the particular order and structure that it has.

We must distinguish between what has been called the "Principle of Sufficient Reason" and the "Principle of Causality." The Principle of Sufficient Reason assumes:

(1) *Nothing occurs without there being a sufficient reason for its occurring.*

We do search for reasons for events and for the properties things have. The Principle of Causality would accept this provided that these reasons are seen in the context of causal phenomena *in* the Universe. The Principle of Causality would rephrase (1) thus:

(2) *If a thing occurs, we then should be able to give a sufficient reason for its occurrence.*

1. From Gottfried Wilhelm von Leibniz, *Monadology and Other Philosophical Essays,* translated by Paul Schrecker and Anne Martin Schrecker, copyright © 1965, by The Bobbs-Merrill Company, Inc., pp. 153–54, reprinted by permission of the publisher.

The Principle of Causality avoids the commitment to there being a sufficient reason for a thing's occurrence *independent* of the sufficient reason we have given to explain it. Sufficient reasons can be found for all things that occur, but for the Principle of Causality this does not mean that there is any further sufficient reason for that sufficient reason or explanation. The Principle of Causality states that all events have causes and these causes are the explanations for those events. The Principle of Causality does not contain an element of "necessity"—that this is the way the event had to happen, and that there was something causing it to happen the way it did rather than another way.

The Principle of Sufficient Reason also assumes:

(3) For all things that exist, it must be possible to give a reason why they exist the way they do rather than in some other way.

For the Principle of Causality, stating the reasons for the occurrence of an event in terms of other interconnected phenomena that are causally related to it is giving "the reason why" they exist the way they do. They do not exist some other way because if they exist the way they are, then that is the way they are and they could not be otherwise. If they were otherwise, then they would be that "otherwise."

The extent to which the Principle of Causality used the phrase "sufficient reason," it would say that each and every part of the Universe has its sufficient reason for being the way it is. This can be found in a causal analysis of some sort (Why-How? or Why-Why?). This aspect of the Universe which serves as the sufficient reason then has its sufficient reason in some other part, and so on ad infinitum. For the Principle of Causality "brute facts" or "ultimates" are that:

(a) there is always something in Existence in some way.

(b) there is always some other contingent event which exists to which we can refer to find sufficient reasons for an occurrence,

(c) there is no Absolute Sufficient Reason. There are only sufficient reasons which are relative to other sufficient reasons.

For the Principle of Sufficient Reason, there must be something outside the phenomena of cause and effect, *outside* the series of contingent events, which is the Cause and the Sufficient Reason for the occurrence of these events, which needs no further sufficient reason for itself, and which is the reason of its own existence. The Principle of Sufficient Reason rejects the Principle of Causality as being insufficient and incomplete whenever it does not appeal transcendently to God but only to the finite series that occur *within* the Universe.

We see that the Principle of Sufficient Reason shares the persistent tendency found in all the other arguments for God's existence:

(i) to see the Universe as a "Whole" or from a position *supra* to its Infinity

(ii) to escape an infinite regress and stop at something final, certain, ultimate, which is a Being

(iii) to make that Being the Transcendent and Sustaining Cause of all that is, thereby providing a Sufficient Reason and

(iv) by providing a Sufficient Reason of this kind for the Existence of the Universe, the question "Why are things the way they are (rather than being some other way)" then is supposedly answered.

6.2   *The Statement of the "Problem."*

Copleston: . . . First of all, I should say, we know that there are at least some beings in the world which do not contain in themselves the reason for their existence. For example, I depend on my parents, and now on the air, and on food, and so on. Now, secondly, the world is simply the real or imagined totality or aggregate of individual objects, none of which contain in themselves alone the reason for their existence. There isn't any world distinct from the objects which form it, any more than the human race is something apart from the members. Therefore, I should say, since objects or events exist, and since no object of experience contains within itself the reason of its existence, this reason, the totality of objects, must have a reason external to itself. That reason must be an existent being. Well, this being is either itself the reason for its own existence, or it is not. If it is, well and good. If it is not, then we must proceed farther. But if we proceed to infinity in that sense, then there's no explanation of existence at all. So, I should say, in order to explain existence we must come to a being which contains within itself the reason for its own existence, that is to say, which cannot not-exist.[2]

---

2. Bertrand Russell, *Why I Am Not a Christian,* edited with an appendix on the Bertrand Russell Case by Paul Edwards (London: Allen & Unwin, 1957), pp. 145–46. Used by permission of the publisher. This is taken from a 1948 BBC debate between Father F. C. Copleston, S. J., and Bertrand Russell.

Russell: So it all turns on the question of sufficient reason, and I must say you haven't defined "sufficient reason" in a way that I can understand—what do you mean by sufficient reason? You don't mean cause?

Copleston: Not necessarily. Cause is a kind of sufficient reason. Only contingent being can have a cause. God is His own sufficient reason; and He is not cause of Himself. By sufficient reason in the full sense I mean an explanation adequate for the existence of some particular being.

Russell: But when is an explanation adequate? Suppose I am about to make a flame with a match. You may say that the adequate explanation of that is that I rub it on the box.

Copleston: Well, for practical purposes—but theoretically, that is only a partial explanation. An adequate explanation must ultimately be a total explanation, to which nothing further can be added.

Russell: Then I can only say that you're looking for something which can't be got, and which one ought not to expect to get.[3]

We have seen that there is no event (or cause or motion) that is not just as contingent as any event we are examining. But the argument continues into another area: If the Universe is to be fully explained, that is if the Universe is to be made fully intelligible, we must at some point arrive at a Necessary Being—a Being that is not contingent like the rest but upon which all the rest depend for their existence, a Being that is Absolutely Necessary needing nothing else to explain It, a Being that is Its own explanation and the explanation of everything else.

It is held that accounting for individual members of a serial chain of causes or motions in terms of an Infinite Regress does not ultimately explain why anything is as it is rather than being another way. All you have is an endless regress of explanations. To fully explain the Universe you have to come to an overall, all-encompassing explanation which explains everything, which explains why everything is the way it is. Contingent things are things that might-not-have-existed. We certainly *can* conceive of the Universe being entirely different from what it is. And why isn't it? If each contingent event is made intelligible by reference to other contingent events, then behind this complexity of events there must be a self-explanatory Necessary Being. Reference to It then would presumably explain everything—the whole scheme of things.

Does the God concept, the concept of a Necessary Being, explain why everything is the way it is? Does the God concept provide an all-encompassing explanation which explains everything? What does it explain and how does it function as an explanation? Is there any necessity to

---

3. Ibid., p. 150.

assume a self-explanatory Necessary Being reference to which everything is made intelligible? What does "self-explanatory" mean? Could the Universe be a "brute fact" requiring no reference to a Necessary Being? Could it be that the Universe just *Is*? What is inadequate about causal explanation given in terms of merely an endless infinite horizontal series of contingent events?

The word "Being" in the phrase "Necessary Being" brings with it connotations of "agency" which are not present in the premises of arguments such as these. Even if one found something which "contained its own reason for its existence," which "contained the explanation of its existence within itself," it would be an unsupported jump to attribute powers of an agency or being to it such as we do in the concept of God as a "Necessary Being." Phrases such as "reason for its own existence," "explanation of its own existence within itself" have nothing to do with causality, with the concept of a *cause*. The Universe itself may be considered to be "its own reason for existing," "its own explanation for being," but this does not in any way make it a causal entity producing effects or serving as an active ground for existence.

The type of intelligibility which the argument for God as the Necessary Being desires is one where there would be no reference to an "ultimate brute fact." Yet the argument itself leads us to this very view of a Necessary Being which is "its own reason for being," which is "self-explanatory," which "just *Is*.' God in the last analysis becomes—must be—a brute fact.

If we accept the position that we can only understand finite aspects of the Universe's Infinite Existence, and never its Infinite Existence (nor even its characteristic as a "Whole"), this does not lead us to the conclusion that the Universe is unintelligible and that only the assumption of a God can make it intelligible. The Universe Itself as a brute fact or as an ultimate is made intelligible the extent to which we can understand conceptually what is meant by such things as its Infinite character, its All-Inclusiveness, its Eternality and its being a final reference beyond which no further reference need be made for the explanation of contingent events. This is what is meant by saying that the Universe is intelligible as opposed to saying that "there is a Necessary Being that makes the Universe intelligible." There is nothing unintelligible about saying that the Universe Itself is Something that can be made sense of, or can be made intelligible but not in the same way that anything in it can be made sense of. The Universe is just an Existence which we make intelligible in some way or other to ourselves. By finding reasons in it for the occurrence of things we make it intelligible and make it rational. The Universe can be made intelligible without there being a Necessary

Being who makes the Universe intelligible for us, or to us. Any thing can be intelligible without something existing to make it intelligible to us.

Saying that every event, every thing in the Universe is *contingent*, that it depends on something outside itself to be explained, is not the same as saying that that *outside itself* source for its explanation is a Transcendent Cause or something *outside the contingent series* in which that event is found. Every event must depend on something outside itself for its explanation, but this need not be something outside the Universe that serves as a cause.

All the major characteristics given to a Necessary Being such as:

(1) Something which "exists by its own nature";

(2) Something which is not perishable;

(3) Something which is not dependent upon anything else *for anything,* not even its own existence;

(4) Something which is *impossible* that it should *not* exist;

can be applied to the Universe as such.

6.3 What Does "Ultimate" or "Complete" Explanation Mean?

The general argument in the previous chapter (V) was of this form: If there are contingent things in the Universe, then there must be a Necessary Being (a Sustaining Cause). There *are* contingent things in the Universe. Therefore, there must be a Necessary Being. In this chapter, the general argument can be put into two similar logical forms (1) and (2) below:

(1) If there is an ultimate or complete explanation of the Universe, then this must be in terms of a Necessary Being (the sufficient Reason for Existence). There *is* an ultimate, or complete explanation of the Universe. Therefore, there must be a Necessary Being.

If the necessity of an ultimate explanation can be denied, the conclusion that there is a Necessary Being would be unacceptable. And if an ultimate explanation can be found, it could still be denied that it need be in terms of a Necessary Being.

We have been looking at the evidence for the existence of a Necessary Being who serves as the ground for the *possibility* of *having* explanations for things, and this ground is simply an *Existing Universe*, but not a Necessary *Being*. Assuming that the Necessary Being is self-explanatory, that you cannot ask for its own ground, merely shifts the location of an ultimate brute fact from the Universe to a God.

> (2) If there is an explanation of *why things are the way they are rather than another way*, then there must be a Necessary Being (the Sufficient Reason for Existence). There is an explanation of *why things are the way they are rather than another way*. *Therefore*, there is a Necessary Being.

We see the interrelatedness of (1) and (2). They presume that an "Ultimate" or "Complete" explanation in terms of a Necessary Being will answer and is the only way to answer such questions as:

> (a) *Why does the Universe Exist rather than there being Nothingness?*

This question is meant to cover other similar questions such as: "Why is there anything at all?" "Why does the Universe Exist?" "Why is there a Universe rather than there being simply *Nothing* at all?" "Why shouldn't there just be *Nothingness?*" "Why should there be anything other than God?" But now, "Why should there even be just a God Existing rather than *Nothing* at all?"

> (b) *Why does the Universe Exist the Way it does rather than some other way?*
>
> (c) *Why are individual things the way they are rather than being some other way?*

In other chapters we have already pointed out the difficulties involved whenever (a) is answered in terms of a God or Necessary Being. Whenever we answer (b) in terms of a God we get similar problems. Why did (or does) God choose this Universe to be what it is rather than having chosen another one? We shall deal specifically with God's "choosing" this Universe "rather than another possible one" in 6.9.

A request for an Ultimate or Complete explanation in terms of a Necessary Being is different from a request for an ordinary explanation. Reference to a Necessary Being does not refer to an explanation of individual things in the Universe but to an explanation of the Universe. This must be done without reference to things *in* the Universe but to some Sustaining or Transcendent Cause—something distinct from the interrelatedness of individual things. Thus it is an explanation *of* the Universe in contrast to an explanation of things *in* the Universe.

This pursuit is based on the assumption that the Universe itself needs an explanation and that there is one. But the Universe does not demand explanation. It does not need an explanation as do events in it such as the formation of the moon, or the breaking of a vase, or the budding of a rose bush, or the first gasp of a child. The request for an ultimate explanation of the Universe also assumes that every ordinary explanation which can satisfactorily make things in the Universe intelligible is to be regarded as not completely adequate.

6.4 What Is an "Explanation"? One always explains something in terms of something else. This is the essential characteristic of "explanation." For example, the rusting of a metal is explained in terms of the oxygen in the air and how it combines with the metal in a chemical process called oxidation. What would it mean to say that there is something which can be explained in terms of *itself alone?* If the definition of "explanation" is to refer to other related conditions, if it is to refer to something *other* than the thing to be explained, then we are *contradicting* our accepted meaning when we say that there is something which is its *own* explanation and need not refer to anything else other than itself. A God that is a Necessary Being, like a Universe that is a Necessary Existent, need not have to be explained—they cannot "help but *Be"*—but this should not be confused with saying that they "have their own explanation only within themselves." There may even be Ultimate Laws which need *not* be explained in terms of any further Laws in an endless regress. These Laws would serve as the means or *source of explanation* for all other things, but again this is not the same as saying that they are self-explanatory or contain their own explanation. They serve as the fundamental starting point for an explanation of a finite aspect of the Universe.

Explanation in the ordinary sense describes the causal conditions of an event and/or establishes some kind of correlation between the event and other events. It tells us *How* the event occurred, under what conditions it occurred, and under what conditions we can expect it to occur. Explanation in the ordinary sense explains what a thing is like in the world and what it was like and what it might be like in the future. If an ordinary causal explanation were inadequate or deficient this would not be corrected by referring to a Necessary Being.

We normally are content to say that an explanation is "sufficient," "satisfactory," "adequate," or "complete" when we can provide some analysis of this sort. Analyses of this sort are what makes the event intelligible to us. Normally we are content with an explanation of an event even though we have not given a complete account of all the possible factors that were related to and involved in that event. Nor do we normally demand that an explanation of an event include reference to any Necessary Being, or to things that are not contingent. We do not consider our explanation to be deficient or incomplete or inadequate because no mention is made of a Necessary Being. We *do* consider our explanation to be deficient if the contingent events which were relevant were omitted. We can insist that there are explanations which are "incomplete," "deficient," or not "ultimate," yet still can be regarded as true and satisfactory explanations whereby things are made intelligible to us.

But ignoring the circularity involved in saying that ordinary explanations are incomplete because they do not refer to a Necessary Being, there are ways in which ordinary contingent explanations are incomplete and not ultimate. Explanations will always be found which are fragmentary, incomplete, and not related to other types of explanations of other types of phenomena. There are many legitimate questions about which we as yet have no answers, at least no satisfactory answers. There will always remain a realm of unanswered questions and of things that have not been explained. If the Universe is an All-Inclusive Infinite then there will always be some things for which there is not as yet an explanation. (This does not imply that there are things which are in themselves inexplicable—merely that there cannot be an explanation for everything.) There will always be a remainder that will remain unexplained. Explanation must be incomplete if only in the sense that all explanations must stop their function somewhere within an infinite number of events to be explained.

6.5   *"Why-How?" and "Why-Why?" Questions and the "Why?" of These.* Some questions *about* the Universe are unintelligible and illegitimate, such as: Where is the Universe? What space is the Universe in? When is the Universe as it is? At what time was the Universe Created? Why has the Universe existed as long as it has from its Beginning? Why has the Universe existed eternally?

There are an infinite number of questions about things in the Universe that can be asked intelligibly and legitimately. *Why* did George Washington cross the Delaware? *Why* does wood burn? *Why* is grass green? *Why* did Dad leave Mom? *Why* did the vase break? *Why* does water boil at 212°F. at sea level?

These questions do not always have to be asked with a "why." There are many meanings of "why." But in ordinary questions of this type we are looking for physical explanations, for the conditions and interconnections that are present and influencing the situation to be explained. In short, the "Why" is answered in terms of "How" the thing has come about. Let's call this the "Why-How" answer.

When we ask, "Why is grass green?" we answer in terms of *How* it is the case that it is green—how due to the presence of chlorophyl and the process of photosynthesis and image-formation on our retina and brain a green appearance is formed. "Why does water boil at 212°F at sea level?" We explain this in terms of how molecules vibrate at changing temperatures, how atmospheric pressure relates to this, and so on.

When we ask "Why did Dad leave Mom?" or "Why did George Washington cross the Delaware?", we more easily can give an answer in terms of their conscious intentions, aims, desires, aggravations, and purposes, without direct reference to a mechanical or behavioristic physical explanation in terms of a "Why-How" analysis. We can call this a "Why-Why" type of answer,[4] although every "Why-Why" explanation in terms of purposive deliberation also can be explained in terms of "Why-How."

It would be foolish to expect a "Why-Why?" answer from some situation that does not contain consciousness or goal-oriented activity. (For some philosophers it is foolish to attempt to explain a goal-oriented activity in terms only of a "Why-How" question.) We have to be careful how we frame our questions because some of them tend to make us answer anthropomorphically. For example: "*Why* is Muller's illusion an illusion?" "*Why* does an acorn become an oak tree?" *Why* does oxygen burn?" "*Why* do human embryos develop in nine months?" In questions such as these we can easily slip from a "Why-How" to a "Why-Why" when there is no real answer in terms of any "Why-Why."

The request for an Ultimate or Complete explanation in terms of a Necessary Being is neither a "Why-How" nor a "Why-Why" request. It is a request for the "Why" of the "Why-How" and the "Why-Why." It is not "Why is grass green?" It is "Why is there green grass?" We can explain the complex chemical reasons and physiological-psychological reasons why grass is green. But the "Why" of an Ultimate explanation in terms of a Necessary Being insists on an answer to the question "Why does *that* chemical process which makes grass green exist—why doesn't some other process exist instead? Why does this particular chemical process make grass green rather than purple?" The interest is not in *How* something comes about, but in *Why* that *How* is the way it is. The interest is not in the mechanics of *How* water boils

---

4. There is a second-type of "Why-Why?" explanation in which there is no direct reference to conscious deliberation although references are made to purposes and functions and ends. For example, we give questions such as "Why does the University of Western Ontario exist?" "Why does the Church exist?" "Why does the labor union exist?" answers in terms of the causal and historical antecedents to their existence and/or in terms of their purposes, functions, activities, and goals. We do this often independently of any reference to human consciousness bringing them into existence. Note that in even this kind of explanation we are staying within the confines of what is—the conditions operating in the situation.

at 212°F but *Why* it does that rather than boil at 100°F at sea level, or "Why" it boils *at all*. The interest is not in Why-How wood burns, but Why is there wood? Why does oxygen burn *rather than* put out fire? Why do these things have the properties they do?

But explaining something by determining "Why-How" (or "Why-Why") a thing has come to exist the way it does answers the question of "Why a thing exists the way it does exist rather than another way." Because it has this existence, and this explanation, it is then what it is rather than something else. Once it has become what it is, it is what it is rather than being something else, and has to be that rather than something else! (Principle of Identity.) Why is grass green? It just is green, that's all (if it is green). That grass is green rather than blue is a brute fact. That grass is the color it is rather than being another color is a brute fact. Why does that chemical process occur to produce green rather than purple or blue? It just does occur and that is all there is to it. Why are things the way they are? Because that is what they have become. Why are things just the way they are, rather than being some other way? Because that is the way they are!

It is always possible to ask *Why a given thing exists rather than another*. Even if we could determine that something else does exist in its place rather than it, we could still ask the same question. (If grass were purple, you could have asked the same question about *that* color.) The oddity is that we can ask this question of *any* and *all* situations without discrimination. This kind of quest leads us nowhere—except to the admission that the Universe *is* what it is because it is. Things in the Universe are made intelligible by means of explanations. But explanations cannot make the Universe itself as a whole intelligible in the same way. Nor is there any need to.

6.6 *Is There an "Ultimate" Explanation Which Itself Requires No Further Explanation?* Two positions can be argued with reference to an Ultimate explanation for the Universe without assuming a Necessary Being:

(1) That there will *always* be something *in* the Universe itself, or something *about* the Universe itself, which does *not* require any explanation in the ordinary sense of explanation—which is a Necessary Existent. It can be argued that at any given time there will *always* be certain structures of the Universe which do *not* depend for their existence on any events in the Universe. These structures are *Eter-*

nally Permanent. They remain as nondependent, permanent structures. Examples of this might be: the atoms themselves; an Infinite structure of the Universe; its Space-Curvature; the velocity of light; distribution of mass; quanta jumps; the laws of gravity.

or   (2) that there *never will be* anything *in* the Universe, which does not have an explanation in the ordinary sense of explanation. At any given time there will *never* be structures of the Universe which do not depend for their existence on any other structures already in existence. There are relatively permanent structures for a time in the Universe which themselves change but do *not* remain as nondependent structures over a period of time. Examples of this might be: Material substances maintain the kind of existence they have because of molecular forces that bind molecules, and nuclear forces that bind nuclei, and so on. The subatomic bonding forces themselves may be different in time. Given enough time there may be entirely different forces acting in the Universe than are present at any given time. There is never any ultimate structure to the Universe which remains the same. There is never anything in such an Infinite Universe at any given time that is not dependent for its existence on some other existing thing in that Universe. There might be more or there might be less sand on the beaches, but it would not be correct to say that the gravitational laws covering the formation of sand on the beaches are what they are regardless of anything else, and *must* and *will always be* what they are and not anything else. There might be more or there might be less humans than there are now in existence, but the laws covering propagation would not eternally be what they are.

Will our explanations of the Universe ever reach an end? Will we arrive at One explanation that explains everything in the Universe? If we did arrive at an Ultimate, Final Law to explain the processes of the Universe, would we be able to recognize it as an Ultimate or Final Law? Would our explanations in terms of general physical laws be different over a long span of time? (Would this not especially be the case if Laws were descriptive statements of processes as opposed to prescriptive?) Or will our explanations reach some permanent Ultimate, Final Law which never changes, and which can at *any time* in Eternity be used to explain all phenomena? If we could find an Ultimate or Final Law to account for the processes in the Universe would this be the same as God the Necessary Being? Would such a Law need to be referred to a Necessary Being? If such a Final Law were found would it need any further explanation? Would it be a basic Law in the sense that it would require no explanation for Itself, but like primitives in mathematics and logic it would provide a reference and beginning point for the explanation of all other phenomena? If the Universe did have Ultimate Laws then they would be Laws that are underived from any other Laws, and we could not ask "Why do *these* Laws 'govern' the Universe rather than there being *other* ones to 'govern' the Universe?"

If we arrived at such Ultimate, underived Laws (or Law) and we could determine that we had arrived there, then it would be self-contradictory to ask for an explanation of *those* Laws. They would not *need* any explanation. They would not have any explanation themselves, yet they would be *used* for an explanation of all other things. If these Laws were so basic and Ultimate there would be nothing further for them to be explained in terms of. To ask for an explanation of them would be self-contradictory.

In a similar fashion asking the question "Why is the Universe the way it is?" is self-contradictory if there is nothing other than the Universe in terms of which we can explain it. If there is no such other then the answer would be: "The Universe is the way it is because that's the way it has become. The Universe is the way it is because that's the way it *is*." In a similar fashion asking the question "Why is the Universe the way it is rather than another way?" is self-contradictory if there is nothing other that the Universe *can be* at any given moment except what it is.

6.7 *Why Do Things Exist the Way They Do Rather Than Some Other Way?* In previous chapters we concentrated on the definition of the Universe as "Everything That Is." This was meant to incorporate two other definitions. We can extend that definition and define the Universe as "Everything that was (Infinitely) and Is." We can further expand even this definition and define the Universe as "Everything that Was (Infinitely) and Is and Will Be (Infinitely)."

The Universe as it is *Now* was *not* the *only* possible Universe. (But the Universe as it is Now is the only Universe possible *Now*.) The Universe as it was at any given time *was not* the *only* possible Universe. What the Universe might be at any given time in the future need *not* be that, but could be otherwise. (What the Universe *will* be at any given time in the future will be that and not otherwise at that moment that it is what it has become.)

It is possible that a particular Universe identical to this one except in one minor respect could have existed, or could exist. It is possible that a particular Universe completely different from this one could have existed, or could exist. It is possible that a particular Universe could exist without me. It is possible that a Universe exists with the Gods of Olympus, with mermaids and satyrs. Another particular Universe is possible whether or not it can be imagined provided its description is *not* self-contradictory.

A particular Universe that had me in it and did not have me in it at a given moment in time would *not* be possible. A particular Universe that was as it was and at the same time and in the same respect was not what it was would not be a possible Universe. Any particular Universe containing square-circles, round-squares, hairless hairs, and a timeless time would *not* be a possible Universe.

The Universe as it is at any particular moment *is* the only possible Universe since that is the one that *Is*, or has come about at that time in an Infinite Time. It is the only real or actual Universe at that moment, and at that moment no other one is possible (and if another one were realized at that given moment then that one would have been the only possible one). In this kind of analysis we do not have the question: "Why of all the infinity of possible Universes, do we have just this Universe rather than another possible one among the infinity of possible ones?"

It is necessary that only one particular Universe be possible at any given moment in time and that is the one that is actual or real at that moment. But this particular "only one" is not necessitated—another particular Universe was possible at that moment in time. We can say: *That Something Exist in Some Way or Other is Necessary.* But this is not the same as saying—and does *not* imply:

(1) that there is a *necessary* thing or structure in the Universe;

(2) that there is a *necessity* for things to happen in the Universe the way they do happen;

(3) that the Universe as a Whole is a *Necessary Being* (It could well be a Necessary *Existent*);

(4) that there is a *Necessary Being*.

Saying that "something else could have been the case," "another particular Universe could have been," "another particular Universe was possible at that moment," and so on is *not* the same as saying that "anything is possible in the Universe at any given time" or "any particular Universe is possible at any given moment in time." When we see some things in a particular Universe being what they are, we then can have a general sense of what, relative to these things, it is not possible to have as a particular Universe following that one. In a general sense we can say what, relative to these things, it is somewhat probable that we will have as a particular Universe following that one.

There is nothing in the Universe that necessitates things to happen the way they do. It is possible that another particular Universe could have happened, but this possibility at any given moment is relative to the Universe as it was. Given a particular Universe with things having happened as they did we can then in general understand why only some possibilities will become realities in the next stage relative to the realities and possibilities that have occurred. If there is any necessity in the Universe it is not a Being that necessitates things to happen, but the necessity of there being possibilities relating in an interconnected framework where not anything can happen at any time in any way. In discussing teleology in the next chapter, we shall see that this kind of order is one of the brute facts or undeniable ultimates of Existence.

There is only one particular Universe about which we can say: *It is as it is and cannot be any other way than it is*—and that is the Actual Universe happening at any given Now. But there is no particular Universe (at any other time than the Now) about which we can say: It is as it is and could never have been any other way, or at another time, than it is, if other things had been different. There is no particular Universe at any time about which we cannot say: It *could* have been other than it is, and *would* have been other than it is, if things had been different—and things *could have* been different. Why isn't the Universe entirely different from what it is? The moment it *is* that Universe, then it *can't* be entirely different from what it is. Its being what it is is limited by what it *was*. It could have been—and we could say it is in the *process of becoming*—"entirely different from what it was."

Every particular thing in the Universe *might not have existed*, or might have existed differently, than what it is. We have seen that this is what is meant by "contingent existence." (This is *not* saying that Nothing-at-all-might-have-existed.) Had conditions been different then *that* particular thing might not have existed as it is, or might not have existed at all. If my mother and father had not met as they did I would not be here. If my mother had not become pregnant when she did, I wouldn't be here. If we had moved from Canada earlier than we did, I would now be a different person in some ways.

When one particular Universe out of many possibilities is realized at any given moment in time, a sufficient reason can be found for its occurrence. This sufficient reason is in terms of the interrelated causes that have operated in the Universe which give us some insight into the possibilities that might come about relative to what have come about. But this sufficient reason is not a reference to a Transcendent Cause or Necessary Being which explains *Why* things exist and *Why* they happen the way they do "rather than another way."

6.8 If You Can't Answer "Why Does the Universe Exist?" Is Then the Universe Irrational, and an Accident or a Chance Event?

We have argued that there is an answer to the question "Why does the Universe Exist?" That the Universe is Eternal without an Absolute Beginning-Point is an answer to that question. We have argued that there is an answer to the question "Why does the Universe exist the way it does rather than some other way?" and to its allied questions. Simply put, the Universe could have been otherwise than it is, but at any given moment in time it is what it is and has to be that rather than something else (since at the time it is what it is it cannot be anything else). We have argued that the question "Why does the Universe Exist rather than there being *Nothingness?*" does not pose a proper set of options and is therefore an illegitimate question. The question "Why does the Universe Exist?" we have seen may mean "What is its meaning or purpose or reason for being here?" and we treated this in 4.9.

So in a sense the question titling this section has to be put into another context if we are to try to come to grips with it fairly. Let us assume that we do not have an answer to "Why does the Universe Exist?" Does this imply then that the Universe exists by accident or chance, that the Universe is Irrational, that the Universe is Meaningless?

Within the Universe we can designate such alternatives. *Within* the Universe we can say that things happen, or exist by chance, by accident, with intent, with deliberate planning, due to ignorance, due to luck, and so on. We can say of things *in* the Universe that they are irrational, that they don't make sense, that they are meaningless (or that they are rational, make sense, have meaning). The Universe itself is not one of these processes or events that happen which can be described in these ways. The Universe is not that sort of entity which is created or produced or made. Therefore these possible designations do not apply to the Universe itself. The Universe is not any "thing" or "happening" which can happen by accident, chance, or luck.

6.9 Does God "Choose" Things to Happen the Way They Do in the Universe?

A major presupposition running through all of the Arguments for God's existence is this: In the final analysis we must see that everything that happens as it does, happens because God *Wills*

it to happen the way it does, God *Chooses* it to happen the way it does.
Science studies merely the effects of this Choosing.

This is in essence another way of theistically answering the question
"Why are things the way they are rather than another way?" Here are
some of the obstacles in this position:

(1) We cannot intelligibly use the words "choose," "decided,"
     "willed" until we can say what real alternatives there are
     in a given situation from which a choice or decision can
     be made.

(2) Again we have the problem of explaining God's wishes,
     choices, decisions, willings. Why—and How—does God
     make the decisions about having just this Universe exist
     of all the possible ones? We can like Leibniz and others
     claim that God, the Necessary Being, Chose or Willed
     this particular Universe to be as it is because of all the
     infinitely possible Universes He could have chosen, He
     regarded this one to be the Best. This is the best choice
     that could have been made. This is the Best of All Possible
     Worlds. (There is a difference between "this actual Uni-
     verse being chosen by God is the Best of All Possible
     Worlds" and "this actual Universe being the best possible
     because it is the only one actual and hence at that time
     the only one possible.") Or we can claim that the reason
     God Chose, or Willed, this Universe of all the other
     possible ones is inscrutable, unknown and unknowable,
     unfathomable—but He did have reasons nevertheless. The
     Ways of God are not the ways of man.

(3) Choices, willings, and decisions themselves have causes.
     If God "chooses" then what is the cause of this choice?
     We are only familiar with choices or willings made by
     existing contingent humans. Can we apply this kind of
     limited description to a God who is doing this on a Cosmic
     level?

(4) In ordinary meanings of "choice," "will," and "decide"
     we have reference to some conscious, intelligent agent
     performing this function. Is God a Supreme Personality
     or Intelligence able to engage in such functions? We are
     led to the argument from design and God as a Universal
     Mind.

VII

God as the Cosmic Mind

7.1 Introduction. The teleological argument attempts to show that the existence of a Cosmic Orderer, a Universal Intelligence, must be accepted to account for the existence of order, design, and regularities which so clearly exist in the Universe.

One of the ways of expressing the teleological argument shows us the general connection with some of the other arguments for God's Existence:

(1) There is order in the Universe. Only God could produce and sustain this order in the Universe. (If it were not for God there would be Chaos, Disorder in the Universe.) Therefore, God exists as the Cause of the order in the Universe.

There is not much difference between this argument and the arguments for God as Sustaining Cause and for God as Sufficient Reason. God is seen as a Being who gave, and/or gives, form and pattern to all the Universe—all form is dependent upon God—but God's Being and Form is not dependent upon anything outside His Own Nature. God's Form is underived from any other existence. But the teleological argument does not prove a temporal First Cause, or a Creator Ex Nihilo. It supports the proposition that the Universe is the Design of a Cosmic Mind which has Supreme Intelligence and Supreme Power in organizing the material in the Universe according to a Plan. The essential characteristic of the teleological argument becomes more apparent when we see its stress upon *Design for a Purpose* which it sees in most things existing in the Universe. The etymology of the word "teleology" is from the Greek τέλος : which has a variety of meanings: The end sought after; goal; aim; purpose toward which an activity is striving. It can even in context mean the "directedness" of a process toward a state of completion whereby its potential to be what it can become is fully realized. Its potential to be what it can become is determined by witnessing what a thing does most of the time. The other part of the word comes from the Greek λόγος (a word pregnant with philosophic meaning accumulated over two thousand years) as "the study of." Etymologically "teleology" is "the study of the ends which things aim for—the study of purpose."

The teleological argument may be put into two other forms:

(2) There is order in the Universe. All order is the product of a mind. Therefore, the order in the Universe is a product of a Mind.

We may accept the first premise. The second premise is not as indubitable. Some order that we see in the Universe is the result of forethought, intelligence, a mind, planning. How do we substantiate that what exists as order outside of that class of "some" is order that also is the product of a Mind? It would be true, if all order in the Universe is a product of a mind, then (any particular) order in the Universe is the product of a mind. But is all the order in the Universe a product of a Mind?

The teleological argument does not need to assert that every thing *at all times* does indeed act orderly, or that all things always can be seen to be in order. All it needs to affirm is that there is some order some of the time and all that order *when it does exist* is due to a mind, to forethought. Another way of putting this is: whenever there is an order, no matter what kind, it can be attributed to a mind. (Is "bad" order also to be attributed to a Mind—to a "Counter-Mind" and a "Counter-Design," like a Satan existing in the Universe? Is "disorder" like cancer to be explained with the same pattern used by the teleological argument?)

The teleological argument has been called the "argument from design." It really should be called the "argument from order" or the "argument from purpose(s)." We may, and do, observe order and purposes in the Universe. But whether this order and these purposes are designed, that is, whether they are the product of a Designer or Cosmic Intelligence, is the question at issue. Can we infer on the basis of accepting the existence of order and purposes in the Universe that there is an Intelligence producing this order? Is this the only possible explanation of this order and these purposes? There may be unanimity about the existence of order and purposes in the Universe but is this order due to God's Intelligent Planning or Design? Is there as well an order and purpose to the Universe itself as a whole which is due to God?

The teleological argument also takes on this form:

(3) The Universe as a Whole is an Order. One cannot intelligibly say that everything in the Universe is an order and not say that the Universe itself is not an Order. Therefore, there must be a God who is the cause of this Cosmic Order of the Universe as a Whole.

The teleological argument in this form takes an immense jump from evidence that order and purposes exist in the Universe to the conclusion that the Universe as a Whole has an Order and a Purpose and a Design. Can this jump be supported?

There is a poetic and emotional ground in the teleological argument for God's Existence which is not present as intensely in the other arguments. For most people it is extremely difficult not to relate the order, beauty, design, regularity, adaptation, purposiveness of things in the Universe to some kind of Universal Mind which is the source of these things, just as human minds can be the source of such things. We design, order, plan, organize by means of our intelligence. Similarly there must be a giant Cosmic Intelligence designing, ordering, planning things to be as they are in the Universe. For one who accepts the teleological argument, the alternative to the acceptance of a Cosmic Mind as the cause of the order in the Universe would be the stupendously unpalatable conclusion that this order, beauty, design "merely happened," "just happens to be one of the infinite possible results of the reconstituting processes of the Universe." We see again a relationship with the previous two chapters: The only fully acceptable and adequate explanation of orderly and purposive phenomena in the Universe for the proponent of the teleological argument is in terms of a Cosmic Intelligence who, with forethought, designed and planned the order and purposes which surround us. Anything short of this answer is unacceptable as a complete or real explanation.

In this chapter, we will directly or indirectly be concerned with questions such as these:

(a) Is there order and are there purposes in the Universe?

(b) Is this order and are these purposes independent of our projection of order and purposes upon the Universe? Are they there apart from our consciousness and our reading order into things?

(c) Is order and are purposes always a product of a mind or intelligence? Can they be explained in any other way?

(d) Is design always to be inferred from an order? Can there be design apart from any Designer or Intelligence?

(e) Is there a Cosmic Order or Purpose? That is, is the order in the Universe so interrelated as to be designated in terms of one fundamental kind of Order (and one fundamental Cosmic Orderer) throughout the Universe? The Universe may show signs of order, but does it show signs of design?

(f) Is there an All-inclusive Cosmic Order or Purpose for the Universe as a Whole? How can this be known?

7.2 *Examples Used in Support of the Teleological Argument.* So many examples have been offered in support of the teleological argument that one hardly knows where to begin. Let us start with an example of "Heavens above." To date billions of galaxies have been indicated, each with their own billions of suns, with solar systems numbering in the billions, many with life-forms similar to our own, and many with life-forms inconceivable to us as yet. There is immense power in the Universe; explosions burst upward to 100,000 miles (half the distance from here to the moon) from the surface of the sun which are millions of times greater than the power of the most powerful hydrogen bomb. Everywhere, this massive Universe, from the movement of the most distant galaxies to the eclipse of the sun, the flight of a comet, and the movement of the planets, exhibits an orderly activity described by our physical laws. Consider the fifteen billion years of development of all the species on earth or the intricate structure and complex activity of the deoxyribonucleic acids which make up the genes. All of these things follow orderly, lawful procedures. The evident increase in complexity of the development of evolution necessitates an explanation in terms of a Supreme Intelligence organizing such an (orderly) increase. Consider the evident existence of an immense complexity in the simplest things such as the thousands of millions of molecules in a drop of water. Think of the immense complexity of the simplest molecule which is a hundred-millionth of a centimeter, which is itself about a hundred thousand times as large as one of its components, the electron, which goes round the nucleus in an estimated trillion times in a trillionth of a second. Consider the fantastic organization and complexity of any part of any living or nonliving existent from the development of the human embryo to a grain of sand, from the firing of a neuron to the awareness of beauty or the shedding of a tear. Consider the coordination in animals of sight, smell, hearing, adrenalin and muscular movement. Consider the means of protection from predators afforded to all animals from claws, fangs, camouflage, teeth, speed, and feigning death. Consider salmon resolutely returning thousands of miles to the place of their birth to spawn; homing pigeons returning hundreds of miles to the place of their hatching; the task is endless. Surely not only the Heavens declare the glory of God —*everything does.*

Wood, bricks, stones, cement, and water do not come together by themselves to organize into a house (Aquinas would argue), so too amino acids do not get together to organize into protein structures, the structures into cells, the cells into life, life into a variety of species, and out of that finally Man and Consciousness. There must be a Supreme, Cosmic Mind at work.

If God indeed did Order and Design the Universe then we should be able to see some signs of his Supreme Intelligence. The examples we cited in this section are taken to be such signs. But are they signs or are they descriptive examples of that order which does in fact take place? We must be careful not to confuse a long list of *examples* of order, design, or purposiveness with the use of these examples *in an argument* as *evidence* for the existence of a Cosmic Orderer. The examples themselves do not constitute evidence. They would not convince anyone who did not already have a prior belief in this kind of Cosmic Mind. The argument itself should be the important deciding criterion and not the examples of order.

Are there characteristics which we can observe in the Universe (or about the Universe as a Whole) which cannot but be due to a God who so structures things? If there were no human rational minds would God's "signature" upon the Universe be there *to be understood* but not understood by anyone? Is this why God fashions man, so that His Sign(s) of authorship can be known? If there were (or are) other types of living creatures with different kinds of minds, would they read the signature in the same way? Suppose He hasn't, and doesn't want, to sign His signature to It?

In analyzing the teleological argument there is an aspect of it akin to the poetic and emotional. Simply put, there is beauty in the world. (This assumes that beauty is an objective reality to be seen as opposed to a subjective emotional response.) We have aesthetic responses in the world. The Universe must have been designed by the Cosmic Mind for our aesthetic contemplation and satisfaction. We do in fact experience an awe and wonder about the Universe. But this we can do to any and all things in it from the existence of lichen to the existence of distant living creatures. (We also can experience the opposite in terms of ugliness, disgust, nausea, revulsion.) We can experience a communion and even a oneness with things around us. We can feel the Universe to be something akin to us, friendly and attuned to our very being. When these emotions are experienced, they feel good and should not be stifled but developed and nourished for they are part of our happiness and comfort. But these experiences and this awareness need not become worship of a Being that has produced them. These aesthetic experiences do enhance life for some but from their existence one cannot conclude that the Universe was designed in order to produce a human aesthetic, religious, or mystical response. There are aesthetic responses to the Universe, but was the Universe itself Designed for this purpose?

7.3 *What the Teleological Argument Does Not Do.* Before going into the teleological argument in more detail let us point out some of its limitations and some of the things it cannot do. None of the arguments for God's Existence professes to be the only complete argument. One has to see them as being interdependent. None of them professes to give a complete account of the nature of God, but each focuses on one main characteristic. Each of them have shortcomings. What are some of the general and obvious shortcomings of the teleological argument?

We have already pointed out in the first section of this chapter that the teleological argument cannot give support to a God as a Temporal First Cause or Absolute Beginner. Nor can it give support to a God Creating Matter out of Nothing. Our experience of "ordering" is to give shape to pre-existing material, not to create it Ex Nihilo. The teleological argument is intertwined so much with the analogy to human creation of artifacts that Creation Ex Nihilo is too distant a leap to take. The argument does not tell us how God Orders the Universe although we shall demonstrate how an attempt is made to overcome this deficiency with an analysis in terms of Divine Will.

The teleological argument leaves open the question "What Kind of God?" Is the teleological character of the Universe an indication that God is an immanent Force (Theism) or Will functioning within all things in the Universe directing the Order? Is God *Transcendent*—different from and Wholly Other to the Universe (Deism), having laid down the Laws which will Govern the Universe, having made the Universe like a watchmaker makes a watch, and then not intervening but watching it go until it needs rewinding and/or some correction whereby the Laws operating are suspended by God in order to perform the correction (Miracles)?

Once a Designer is assumed, then we see Him as a Being possessing a Mind, Intelligence, Wisdom, Power, Personality, Benevolence, and Values. Most of these properties are already present in our suffix "er" which implies a human-type consciousness in operation. But granting that there is such a Being which is a Mind and a Power, the teleological argument of itself very weakly offers evidence for such a Mind possessing Wisdom, Personality, and Goodness and being Value-directed. The teleological argument must be reinforced with other arguments to make these further claims acceptable. Can this Mind exist without being a Personality? (What meaning would such a concept of "Mind" have?) Can this Mind exist and be Indifferent and not Value-directed and not Benevolent? (We find such personalities in our experiences.)

The teleological argument cannot substantiate without first presupposing that the order in the Universe (and/or the Order of the Universe as a Whole) is due necessarily to one Single Cosmic Designer or Mind. There could be several working in conjunction, or an infinite number, each assigned to one member of the infinite numbers of order present in the Universe.

> But were this world ever so perfect a production, it must still remain uncertain whether all the excellences of the work can justly be ascribed to the workman. If we survey a ship, what an exalted idea must we form of the ingenuity of the carpenter who framed so complicated, useful, and beautiful a machine? And what surprise must we feel when we find him a stupid mechanic who imitated others, and copied an art which, through a long succession of ages, after multiplied trials, mistakes, corrections, deliberations, and controversies, had been gradually improving? Many worlds might have been botched and bungled, throughout an eternity, ere this system was struck out; much labour lost, many fruitless trials made, and a slow but continued improvement carried on during infinite ages in the art of world-making. In such subjects, who can determine where the truth, nay, who can conjecture where the probability lies amidst a great number of hypotheses which may be proposed, and a still greater which may be imagined?
>
> And what shadow of an argument, continued Philo, can you produce from your hypothesis to prove the unity of the Deity? A great number of men join in building a house or ship, in rearing a city, in framing a commonwealth; why may not several deities combine in contriving and framing a world? This is only so much greater similarity to human affairs. By sharing the work among

several, we may so much further limit the attributes of each, and get rid of that extensive power and knowledge which must be supposed in one deity, and which, according to you, can only serve to weaken the proof of his existence. And if such foolish, such vicious creatures as man can yet often unite in framing and executing one plan, how much more those deities or demons, whom we may suppose several degrees more perfect![1]

The teleological argument does not justify any insistence that that Being is Jewish, Christian, Moslem, Hindu, or Buddhist. It establishes no God of any particular sect or religion.

That God which the teleological argument purports to prove cannot be an Infinite Mind or Designer or Intelligence or Orderer. Those phrases would be contradictory. If a Mind is a Mind, if a Being is a Being operating as an Intelligence in the Universe, it can be of vast Power, Intelligence, and Forethought but not in any of these ways Infinite. All of these activities in so far as they are activities mean and presuppose finiteness— finite expression and finite control. This is the context in which they have meaning. The God of the teleological argument can be All-the-Power-that-there-Is and All-the-Intelligence-that-there-Is and the-Sum-Total-of-All-These-things but not the Infinite of each of these things nor the Infinite of all of them.

To use Hume's argument to make this point (found both in his *Dialogues Concerning Natural Religion,* part V, and his *An Inquiry Concerning Human Understanding,* section XI): From any effect we can observe, we can infer an unobserved cause which is only sufficient enough to produce that particular effect—no more and no less. From any given effect we can argue to a given cause that is only as great as that which could produce that effect. We have never observed effects other than finite effects. We thus cannot infer an Infinite Cause. (Even though there may be infinite effects occurring at any given moment in the Universe, this does not necessitate an Infinite Cause, but an infinity of causes correlated with this infinity of effects.) So the Design in the world which we actually observe may be of remarkable variety and proportions far superior to anything our Mind could construct. Nevertheless it is all seen as a finite Design, and this does not allow us to conclude that the Cosmic Designer or Mind is an Infinite Designer or Infinite Mind. Nothing in the effect (Design, Order) necessitates or illustrates an Infinite Designer or Mind. We can add our previous point that nothing in the concept of *cause* for a design necessitates or illustrates an Infinite Designer or Infinite

---

1. David Hume, *Dialogues Concerning Natural Religion,* edited by Henry D. Aiken (New York: Hafner, 1948), p. 39. Used by permission of Macmillan Publishing Co.

Mind. The same kinds of arguments would apply if one referred to God as Absolute Infinite Goodness or Infinite Spirit or Infinite Being.

Also the teleological argument in itself does not show that the Designer still exists. As Michael Scriven has put it:

> And even if it had at one time existed, there would be no reason why it should exist any longer, no reason to think that it must be good, or powerful enough to intervene in the workings of its design once it has been set going, or able to foresee the outcome of its designing activities. In short, a Designer is not the same as God, and the Teleological Argument lends no support at all to the claim that there was a Designer.[2]

The teleological argument does not state What the Purpose is nor describe the Order of the Universe—apart from the orders and purposes which we do in fact find. Words such as purpose and order with reference to the Universe remain meaningless and without content unless the purpose and order is specified. Is everything in the Universe directed toward the fulfillment of values which we cherish, toward the perfection of man, and the achievement of God's Will? Is there—or can we have—any indication of this? What about the existence of evil, pain, and suffering in the Universe? Is this to be taken as an indication that these things in the Universe were not Designed by a Designer who is All-Good, All-Wise, and All-Powerful?

7.4 The Teleological Argument as Found in Aquinas: The Fifth Way.

The fifth way of Aquinas' Five Ways to prove God's Existence is the teleological way. There are other teleological arguments in the works of Aquinas but the only other one we shall examine will be from the *Summa Contra Gentiles* which can be seen to be a good supplement to the Fifth Way found in the *Summa Theologica*. The Fifth Way:

> We see that things which lack knowledge, such as natural bodies, act for an end, and this is evident from their acting always, or nearly always, in the same way, so as to obtain the best result. Hence it is plain that they achieve their end, not fortuitously, but designedly. Now whatever lacks knowledge cannot move towards an end, unless it be directed by some being endowed with knowledge and intelligence; as the arrow is directed by the archer. There-

2. From *Primary Philosophy* by Michael Scriven, p. 130. Copyright 1966 by McGraw-Hill Book Company. Used with permission of McGraw-Hill Book Company.

fore some intelligent being exists by whom all natural things are directed to their end; and this being we call God.[3]

Let us outline the argument and some of its presuppositions:

(1) There are "things which lack knowledge" (such as genes, human bodies, acorns, planets) yet they operate in such a way as to achieve a purpose—they *act for an end.*

(2) This seeking and achieving their end is *not* by *chance* (cannot be blind or fortuitous activity since it is directional activity) but by *design.*

(3) The "things which lack knowledge" yet which aim for an end, purpose, or goal cannot do this on their own, since things which lack knowledge do not have this ability of directional activity.

This is the central element in the argument. Whatever does not have an intelligence of its own cannot "act for an end." It must be directed to that end or purpose by something which has intelligence and forethought: "Now whatever lacks knowledge cannot move toward an end, unless it be directed by some being endowed with knowledge and intelligence; *as the arrow is directed by the archer.*" (Can it be shown that this order must come about only on the analogy of the archer and an intelligence which directs the order to that end result, reaching the mark? Is it a proper analogy?)

(4) Therefore, analogous to the arrow being directed by an archer to its mark, there is an Intelligent Being directing "things which lack knowledge" to their end or purpose. This Being we call God.

For Aquinas to "act for an end" means at least two things which are not clearly distinguished in his argument:

(a) nonintelligent things act for (act toward) ends, purposes, or goals, and

(b) nonintelligent things act always, or nearly always, in the same way, *so as to obtain the best result.* An example of this would be your body coming back to health again after an infection. (Can this striving for "the best result" be explained in terms other than a Cosmic Intelligence

3. Anton C. Pegis, ed., *Introduction to St. Thomas Aquinas* (New York: Random House, 1967), *Summa Theologica,* Q. 2, Art. 3, pp. 24–27. Used by permission of the publisher.

or Mind? Is it true that "bodies act always, or nearly always, in the same way, so as to obtain the best result"?)

When (a) and (b) are seen to be intimately related, the argument seems to gain more strength. It gains more of an intuitive strength when we add a third observation:

(c) "Act for an end" also refers to the regularity, the recurring patterns in the Universe of nonintelligent things on the basis of which we can predict, expect, anticipate, explain intelligently, and eventually control.

How can we account for such things without reference to a Universal Mind ordering things in such a way that we can predict and control things in the Universe? Intelligibility presupposes an Intelligence that has made it intelligible, so predictability and regularity presuppose something that has made that order predictable and regular.

The argument as presented in the *Summa Theologica* does not elaborate (c). Aquinas does enlarge on this point in several other places, such as in the *Summa Contra Gentiles* where he emphasizes this feature of the teleological argument:

. . .The mutual order of all diverse things that are directed to each other is on account of their order towards some one thing: even as the mutual order of the parts of an army is on account of the order of the whole army to the commander-in-chief. For that certain diverse things be united together in some relationship, cannot result from their own natures as distinct from one another, because from this there would rather result distinction among them. Nor can it result from different causes of order: because these could not possibly of themselves as differing from one another have one order in view. Accordingly either the mutual order of many is accidental, or it must be reduced to one first cause of that order, who sets all in order towards the end which he intends. Now, all the parts of this world are observed to be ordered to one another, in so far as certain things are aided by certain others: thus the lower bodies are moved by the higher, and the latter by incorporeal substances, as shown above. Nor is this accidental, since it happens always or for the most part. Wherefore this world has but one director and governor. But there is no other world besides this. Therefore there is but one governor of the universe, and Him we call God.[4]

4. Saint Thomas Aquinas, *The Summa Contra Gentiles*, trans. the English Dominican Fathers (New York: Benziger Brothers, 1924), vol. I, pp. 89-90. Used by permission of the publisher.

Aquinas may be right. It may be the case that we can find in nature things that are ordered to one another. Their order to one another may be for the sake of their order to some "one thing." Perhaps we can explain the activity called genetic coding in this way, or the development of an embryo, or even homeostasis although they have been explained in terms of other models such as feedback mechanisms. But this is not a sufficient ground for saying that there is one first ordering cause that orders all other things to the end it intends. This type of teleological ordering may be inherent and limited only to these particular individual structures of natural bodies which exhibit them, but not to *all* bodies in an interrelated way nor to One Guiding First Order separate from the Universe.

Aquinas' analogy to an army is rather unfortunate since it presupposes the very point for which he is supposed to be presenting evidence. Is it really the case that the Universe is like the order of the parts of an army among themselves is for the sake of the order of the whole army to its commander-in-chief? Does the Universe have a Supreme General? That is the issue to be decided—is there such a Supreme Orderer at the Head of all order? (Not even a Supreme General does all the organizing and ordering. On the basis of the analogy who else is involved in the ordering and organizing? Answers have been given in Christianity to questions such as these with reference to Angels and the λόγοι.)

We can assume that an army was victorious due to the superior forethought and planning of a supreme commander. Or we can assume that the army was victorious by accident, or by stupidity of the opposing army. The latter we have no right to assume if over a long period of time there is victory after victory. Still do we have a right to attribute many victories to one supreme commander? So with the multitude of (unintelligent) natural bodies interacting and cooperating with one another to fulfill purposes—must we attribute these to One Supreme Intelligence?

7.5   On the Cooperation and Coordination of Things to Achieve an End. One of the basic ingredients in the teleological argument is the notion of the marvelous "coordination" and "cooperation" of diverse and divergent things (as Aquinas puts it) in the Universe in order to attain certain ends. Things not only relate, they co-relate. Things not only interact but interact harmoniously and usefully. It is as if things were made to fit with each other in a general pattern: the intricate and complex timing and functioning of the multifarious parts of the eye to produce sight; the existence of milk in the mothering animal's breast to feed the young; water and oxygen to produce and sustain life.

The teleological argument is used to elevate man to the position of being the Highest Good or Highest End toward which all this coordination and cooperation takes place. The Final End is the Perfection of Man.

One of the logical problems in the teleological argument is that it uses such words as cooperate and coordinated in a way that begs the question. The essence of the teleological argument is the reference to the splendid adjustment and adaptation, the fantastic coordination and cooperation, of diverse and divergent things to produce the purpose or end of the whole. The parts of the genes, the parts of the cells, the parts of the eye, the movements of the planets, the presence of oxygen are adjusted, adapted, and coordinated to one another and in such cooperation ends are achieved which otherwise would never be achieved.

But in the teleological argument these words "adjusted," "adapted," "coordinated," and "cooperating" are used to mean "deliberately, consciously with forethought and intelligence put together and directed in order to produce the end intended by the whole." This is question begging, for whether or not these things are so adjusted, adapted, or coordinated in order to achieve an end in this sense is the very question to be answered. Is this adaptation, adjustment, and cooperation we see in things *contrived* or *organized* (by a Being)? Or is there another possibility for their being that way?

Of course if the teleological argument does not use these words in such a question-begging way, then it no longer has anything to base itself on for the words "adapt," "adjust," "coordinated" mean simply that in descriptive fact there are many events which interact, combine, and organize and which again (as a matter of fact) are followed by these other events or effects which are evident. In this sense any re-organization, any directional activity, any complex combination of things which takes place can be said to be adjusted, adapted, or coordinated to produce some purpose or end. Trillions and trillions of complex events cooperate, are adjusted and adapted, to produce life on earth, or the earthquake that kills three million people, or the beautiful red in the sunrise. This coordination, adjustment, cooperation, adaptation is surely no evidence of an intended design by a Designer.

Another problem is that the teleological argument confuses the existence of an effect with the existence of that effect as an *intended end purposed* by some Being. Our earth has oxygen which provides for life. The earth has a protective shield of ozone which prevents hazardous radiation from outer space from killing us off. The earth is just in the proper orbit around the sun for life to occur—a few hundred miles closer to the sun or away from the sun would have made our planet uninhabitable. If we argue that oxygen, the ozone layer, and the earth's orbit were ordered that way to produce an end or purpose (life, man) we are putting the cart before the horse. These are effects. Life and man are developments that occurred in adaptation to these conditions but are not ends *intended* by these conditions or by a Being. Life and man came into existence because of these complex conditions on earth. They were caused by these conditions but the conditions were not *put* there for that purpose.

7.6   Analogy in the Teleological Argument. The teleological argument as presented by Cleanthes in Hume's *Dialogues Concerning Natural Religion* clearly brings out the analogical character of the argument.

> Look round the world, contemplate the whole and every part of it: you will find it to be nothing but one great machine, subdivided into an infinite number of lesser machines, which again admit of subdivisions to a degree beyond what human senses and faculties can trace and explain. All these various machines, and even their most minute parts, are adjusted to each other with an accuracy which ravishes into admiration all men who have ever contemplated them. The curious adapting of means to ends, throughout all nature, resembles exactly, though it much exceeds, the production of human contrivance—of human design, thought, wisdom and intelligence. Since therefore the effects resemble each other, we are led to infer, by all the rules of analogy, that the causes also resemble, and that the Author of nature is somewhat similar to the mind of man, though possessed of much larger faculties, proportioned to the grandeur of the work which He has executed. By this argument *a posteriori,* and by this argument alone, do we prove at once the existence of a Deity and His similarity to human mind and intelligence.[5]

We saw Aquinas draw an analogy between directional order in the Universe and *an arrow aimed at its mark,* and between the overall coordinated order throughout the Universe and an army's unity and victory derived from a chief of staff. Cleanthes' analogy is not essentially different but puts more emphasis on contemplating the Universe as "one great machine, subdivided into . . . lesser machines."

Cleanthes' attempt, like Paley's years later, sees the Universe as being similar to machines that have been designed. Just as these machines (artifacts, contrivances) are designed and produced by man's intelligence, so the Universe is Designed and Produced by a Cosmic Intelligence or Mind. The usual analogy taken from William Paley (1743–1805) is to a watch: We see order in a watch. We know, or at least can easily

---

5. Hume, *Dialogues Concerning Natural Religion,* p. 17. Used by permission of Macmillan Publishing Co.

infer, that this order was produced by the intelligence of a watchmaker. The Order in Nature is like the order in a watch but superior and far more complicated. We can conclude that there is an Orderer like the watchmaker, who is the cause of this Order in Nature, and that is God, the Supreme Intelligence.[6]

We see many similarities between the Order in the Universe and the order in machines. The order in machines is designed by human intelligence. The Order in the Universe also must have been designed by an Intelligence—and an Intelligence of far Superior Abilities and Powers since the Order in the Universe can be seen to be so vastly more intricate and complex.

In the previous sections we discussed the assumption in the teleological argument (which Cleanthes also makes in the above passage) that things in the Universe do have adjustments of parts to parts, of means to ends (such as the directional activity of an acorn or the coordination of the parts of the eye to produce vision) which can only be explained in terms of an intelligence and not in terms of the natural and inherent structures of the orders themselves. In this section we want to examine such assumptions as: that this adjustment or adaptation is like that which we see in human productions (machines, watches, contrivances, artifacts) made by man's intelligence; that this applies to the Universe as a Whole; that the analogy is a good "proof" of a Supreme Intelligence and if not a proof it at least offers us some probable ground for God's Existence.

We should comment about this last point before we proceed. There is a general consensus in logic that analogies do not prove anything. They may offer suggestions. Analogies do not give facts but by their organizing models they may suggest how to go about finding facts. They

---

6. The famous argument from design of William Paley is found in his *Natural Theology or Evidence of the Existence and attributes of the Deity, collected from the Appearances of Nature* (1802). This book was the precursor of the eight Bridgewater Treatises published between 1833–1840 under the auspices of the Royal Society. These books as well as many others before and after Darwin's *Origin of Species* (1859) were written to support the existence of a Supreme Intelligence by citing innumerable examples of design which exist everywhere from man and living creatures to the heavens above. It was a certainty for the authors of these books that the operations of a Supreme Designer could be found everywhere.

Kai Nielsen in his chapter on "The Argument from Design" in *Reason and Practice* (New York: Harper & Row, 1971), p. 185, comments:

". . . Paley's work served as the metaphysical underpinning for many of the scientists who stubbornly and bitterly resisted Darwin in the first years after the publication of the *Origin of Species* (1859). Ironically enough, David Hume's *Dialogues Concerning Natural Religion*, published in 1779—twenty-three years before the publication of Paley's *Natural Theology*—radically and powerfully criticized arguments of the type made by Paley. And it is sad to note that there is little in Paley's argument to exhibit that he was aware of how damaging Hume's criticisms were to his claims. Yet during the nineteenth century, in so far as educated popular consciousness was concerned Paley's arguments carried the day." (Used by permission of the publisher.)

may suggest facts but whether or not they are facts is to be determined by empirical methods.

This is true of analogies that can be formulated. In the case of the analogy in the teleological argument, we do not know (and have no way of finding out) whether there is any analogy or not. To put it more strongly, we can never formulate even the beginning of an analogy. If an analogy is fallacious (has a false premise), we then can argue that it does not prove and does not point to or suggest its conclusion. But if no analogy can even be formulated with reference to God, then it cannot be argued, as some do, that the teleological analogy may not prove God but it certainly points to or suggests some kind of Being behind all the order. Wallace Matson argues this way:

> The second reason for doubting whether the design argument is an analogy is a weightier one. If the argument is an analogy, then it is an extremely weak one—much weaker even than Hume judged, so weak that we must be amazed that anyone could have thought it to have any force whatsoever. For it is in fact at least as weak as the following argument:
>
> Premise I. Natural objects share with artifacts the common characteristic of being colored.
>
> Premise II. Artifacts are colored by being painted or dyed. Conclusion: Therefore natural objects are probably colored by a great painter-dyer.
>
> We take it as self-evident that this is an extremely weak argument, to which no one would assent. Yet it cannot be weaker than the design analogy, because it is of the same form and its premises are obviously true. (It may be objected that the second premise is not true, since some artifacts retain their "natural" colors. I mean, though, that when we know how they got their colors, we know that they got them by being painted or dyed. And, besides, some artifacts retain as components, "natural" adaptation of means to ends: e.g., squirrel cages.) How so weak an argument could seem strong needs accounting for; and I doubt whether cynical references to the unbounded credulity of *homo religiosus* will suffice.
>
> I shall try to explain these anomalies by suggesting that the paint argument is less convincing than the design argument precisely because its premises are more obviously true. From this I shall conclude that the analogical form disguises the real form of the design argument.[7]

---

7. Reprinted from Wallace I. Matson: *The Existence of God*, p. 125. Copyright © 1965 by Cornell University. Used by permission of Cornell University Press.

One of Hume's points in his *Dialogues* is that since the Universe is Unique—a Single All-Inclusive Thing and there are no others of them—we can never draw an analogy between them. According to Hume we can have an analogy when we have comparisons of similarities. In an analogy we must have a set of descriptions of a thing which can be compared against a set of descriptions of some other thing of the same kind. In the case of the Universe we can never experience another thing of the same kind, let alone experience the Universe as a Whole. Since the Universe is Unique we are never able to construct an analogy to another Universe in order to draw the required comparisons to establish an analogy. We are never in a position to say: Universe[1] has these and these qualities which are similar to these and these qualities in Universe [2], Universe [1] has this other additional quality, so therefore since the two are so similar in other respects, Universe [2] probably has this additional quality too. If we knew other Universes and knew how they were created, such as knowing many types of machines and knowing that they were produced by intelligences, then we could construct an analogy and say that this Universe too was probably so constructed because of its close similarity to these other Universes. But we cannot do this with the Universe if the Universe is, and means, All There Is. There are no other Universes to compare this Universe to—even if we could know it as a Whole.

By definition there is only One Universe. Since it is unique even though we might be able to think of it as a "Whole" we cannot include it in any class or species (as Hume puts it) in which we may reason analogically. But can any conclusions about the Universe as a Whole be inferred from some of its parts? Can we argue that parts of the Universe of which we have experience are similar to the functions of machines *and* just as machines were made by intelligence so too the Universe was made by an Intelligence? If we argued this way, we would be reasoning from a part to the whole. We have seen how easily we can fall into the fallacy of composition by arguing this way. But our problem is, can we even say anything about the Universe as a Whole from an examination of its parts *and have it checked?*

In an analogy you must have at least three known things to compare with each other in terms of similarities and relationships, the fourth thing is the possible or probable X, or "inferred conclusion." (I put this last phrase in quotation marks because as we mentioned there are many who do not accept analogical reasoning as a formal method of proof in logic, nor as an inductive form of reasoning leading to any inductive conclusion.) In the case of the teleological analogy three things are not known; only two are known, and, therefore, the analogy cannot work.

We may know about the order in machines. We may know that that order has been made by an intelligence. But we do not know (and cannot infer by reasoning from parts to whole) that the Universe is Ordered like a machine. (Does it have characteristics about it like the order in a machine—cogs, wheels, circuits, springs, cylinders?)

Hume's point here is that if we can use the machine-model to understand the Universe as a Whole, then we find one kind of God in our analogy. But what prevents us from using as our base for the analogy the model of animal procreation (in any of its several varieties), or vegetative generation, or instinct, or artistic creation on a canvas? If we used these analogies (if analogies to the Universe could be drawn), we then would form other slightly different conceptions of God.

Philo in Hume's *Dialogues* says:

> Compare, I beseech you, the consequences on both sides. The world, say I, resembles an animal; therefore it is an animal, therefore it arose from generation. The steps, I confess, are wide, yet there is some small appearance of analogy in each step. The world, says Cleanthes, resembles a machine; therefore it is a machine, therefore it arose from design. The steps are here equally wide, and the analogy less striking. And if he pretends to carry on *my* hypothesis a step further, and to infer design or reason from the great principle of generation on which I insist, I may, with better authority, use the same freedom to push further *his* hypothesis, and infer a divine generation or theogony from his principle of reason. I have at least some faint shadow of experience, which is the utmost that can ever be attained in the present subject. Reason, in innumerable instances, is observed to arise from the principle of generation, and never to arise from any other principle.

> Hesiod and all the ancient mythologists were so struck with this analogy that they universally explained the origin of nature from an animal birth, and copulation. Plato, too, so far as he is intelligible, seems to have adopted some such notion in his *Timaeus*.

> The Brahmins assert that the world arose from an infinite spider, who spun this whole complicated mass from his bowels, and annihilates afterwards the whole or any part of it, by absorbing it again and resolving it into his own essence. Here is a species of cosmogony which appears to us ridiculous because a spider is a little contemptible animal whose operations we are never likely to take for a model of the whole universe. But still here is a new species of analogy, even in our globe. And were there a planet wholly inhabited by spiders (which is very possible), this inference would there appear as natural and irrefragable as that which in

our planet ascribes the origin of all things to design and intelligence, as explained by Cleanthes. Why an orderly system may not be spun from the belly as well as from the brain, it will be difficult for him to give a satisfactory reason.[8]

We could "prove" any kind of God we wanted by shifting our analogy. References to machines, artists, generative processes of animals, vegetative regeneration, and the like may provide some kind of model or general framework by which a lot of things can be understood *in* the Universe, but they cannot and do not provide a model for our understanding of the Universe itself either as a Whole or an Infinite. Consider the many ways in which things in the Universe are *unlike* machines. (On what kind of machines are we to base our analogy since there are a variety of them? Watches, locomotives, computers, nuclear energy plants?) Consider the many ways in which some things in the Universe are unlike vegetables, animals, or an artistic creation. The strength of the analogy is based on the number and strengths of the similarities. With reference to the Universe, questions such as the following cannot even be asked: "Can many similarities be drawn to a machine?" "To which of these models are we going to draw a comparison for the Universe?" "What about the dissimilarities?" The extent to which we present differences determines the extent to which the argument loses its power to be convincing. The point is that none of these models or even any model fits the Universe. They all have their range of application *in* the Universe but do not and cannot apply to the Universe itself.

If we do away with reference to any of these particular models for an analogy and merely refer descriptively to the very existence of Order—all these types of orders and many more that can be seen—then we do not have a teleological argument or a Cosmic Designer.

There is never a time in the Universe at which some kind of order cannot be said to exist. There will always be evidence for the existence of some kind of order in any and all possible Universes. Evidence for the existence of any particular order in the Universe could be different. Any particular order could have been different. Nevertheless the conclusion of the teleological argument that there is a Cosmic Designer or Orderer would not be any different whatever particular order were found. Such a conclusion would be compatible with *any* and *all* kinds and degrees of order. The teleological argument does not depend for its conclusion on any specific kinds of order. *Any* and *all* order can be interpreted by the argument as an illustration of its conclusion that there is a Cosmic

---

8. Hume, *Dialogues Concerning Natural Religion,* pp. 50–51. Used by permission of Macmillan Publishing Co.

Orderer. This has been assumed as a strength of the teleological argument, but it is really one of its weaknesses.

7.7   Is the Order in the Universe Due to an Intelligence or Will?

We can agree that some order which we see in existence in the Universe is relative to us. It depends on how we look at what we are looking at. So with disorder. The order and disorder (or nonorder) we see will vary according to our interests, values, powers of concentration, methods of organizing—in general our perspectives and biological structures. A bee, an ant, or a snake "sees" order differently. We also can agree that some degree of order will be found in anything the mind attends to. Lastly, we might even agree that some order exists independently of human consciousness, some order which we describe, and some of these descriptions are accurate ones of an "order out there." This last point is difficult to substantiate but it seems to be a fundamental viewpoint and a persistent tendency in both common sense and science, that is, that not all order is purely subjective order. If we accept this viewpoint it is difficult to make a definite distinction between what order is relative and/or subjective and what order is objective and out beyond consciousness. Nevertheless, however we judge this problem, there is a difference between saying that the Universe is in some kind of order at any given moment or length of time and saying that the Universe *is an* order.

> . . . (1) The word "order" is not very clear: that which seems orderly to one person will not seem so to another. A painting that appears orderly to one observer will appear chaotic to another. (2) Nor is it clear that the universe is orderly in any specific sense. If galaxies are orderly, but drifting nebulae in the universe are not, then it must be pointed out that there are many nebulae in the universe; and so on for anything that might be considered not to be orderly. Yet if *anything* that the universe contains is orderly, no matter what, then what are the limits on the term "orderly"? What could count against a thing or arrangement of things being orderly? If you throw a bag of marbles on the floor, they must fall out in *some* order or other. In this sense, every arrangement of things must be orderly, so the statement that *this* universe is orderly tells us nothing distinctive about it. (3) Most important, what is the guarantee that order is always the result of design? Some examples of order are indeed the result of design, as in the case of mechanical objects (watches, wrenches, automobiles); we know this because we ourselves (or other human beings) have taken the materials and put them together in certain ways to form objects that we can use and enjoy. The order is there as a result of designing minds—*ours*. But as Hume said, order

is evidenced for design *only* to the extent that order has been *observed* to result from design. And the order we find in plants and animals has not been observed to result from design. We have never seen any beings who form plants or animals, or for that matter stars, as a result of their design, and therefore we are not entitled to conclude that these things do exist as the result of design.[9]

It is impossible to know what is meant when we say that the Universe is *an* Order, or is Ordered or Disordered, unless we can know *in what respect* we expect the Universe to be ordered or disordered. We cannot state the respect in which we expect it to be orderly or disorderly because wherever we go in the Universe we find it in some kind of order (the order that it has), or we put it into some kind of order. We can never have any reason to expect it to have one kind of order or disorder as opposed to another. (What other kind of order or disorder could it have?) We can never specify that the Universe is *an* Order with respect to something else. Since we cannot do this, then saying that the Universe is *an* Order is without meaningful content. The Universe *Is* and it is in some order.

If a Universe exists at all it must be in some order where things in it relate to one another. It will have the property of things coming into an order, coming into patterns. Any Universe, especially one with consciousness in it, will be in some kind of order and will be seen to have the appearance of some kind of order. That the Universe is in some kind of order does not imply a Cosmic Designer. There is nothing that is perceived or experienced which is not in some kind of order. The same applies to the existence of complexity. If the Universe exists at all it will exist in some complexity. The Universe at any time in Eternity will be complex.

It could be argued that if the Universe exists with our degree of complexity in it, if our complexity has come out of the complexity of the Universe, then this in itself illustrates how complex the Universe is and we should expect the Universe to be immensely complex. And why should we expect any Universe not to be complex? What order is not complex except that which has been made simple by means of the simplifications of abstract thought? Thus it also could be argued that nothing is any more complex than anything else. "Complexity" is a relative judgment related to our ability to simplify or not. This would be an important point to keep in mind when arguing that the Universe shows in evolution a progressive increase in complexity. We tend to

9. John Hospers, *An Introduction to Philosophical Analysis*, 2d ed. © 1967, pp. 456–57. Reprinted by permission of Prentice-Hall, Inc., Englewood Cliffs, New Jersey.

think in terms of simple beginning points which develop more and more complexity as time goes on to a point of fulfillment. This may be characteristic of some things in the Universe, or even of all areas in the Universe, but not of the Universe itself as Infinite or as a Whole. Then again if complexity is a relative term can we talk about the increase in complexity from a protoplasm to human consciousness or only about the *development* of human consciousness from protoplasmic material?

One of the things we mean when we say that the Universe is an Order is that we can put some of its patterns into general, abstract but simply understood laws or theories which depict the Universe's general and persistent patterns and relations. We can predict. Things in the Universe are predictable as well as regular and orderly. Things in the Universe are governed by Universal Laws. Things in the Universe obey or follow the Laws which guide the Universe. God is the Designer who has created these Laws by which all things are ordered the way they are in the Universe.

It seems obvious though that things in the Universe can be regular, can be predicted, or are predictable and still may not be due to a Designer or Cosmic Intelligence. Regularity, predictability like directional activity, and coordinating activity can belong as qualities to the Universe itself. They need not in any way be considered as qualities derived from some outside Cosmic Designer who has given them to the Universe in some way.

Our Physical Laws about things in the Universe describe what is happening. It is a further step into the teleological picture which convinces us that physical laws are also prescriptive in the sense of *making* things happen. We use phrases such as "the Reign of Law," "the Universe Ruled by Law or Governed by Law." But we must be careful not to allow the picture in these words to make us suppose the existence of a King, a Lawgiver who exists and who reigns and governs by means of these Laws he has decreed.

We also use phrases such as "the Principle of Uniformity," "the Principle of Order." There is a tendency to hypostatize or reify these terms—to regard them as independently existing entities or beings or causes bringing uniformity and order into the Universe. These phrases merely state that there *is* Uniformity and Order (to be looked for in specific situations), *not* that they *cause* such Uniformity or Order.

We have seen that the important aspect of the teleological argument is not only the existence of *order*, of regularity and of design, but the existence of a *direction*. Something exists to *direct* unintelligent things to an *end*. This something has been identified as an Intelligence or Will. In the analogy of human beings giving direction to their activities and creations by means of intelligence and will, so too God as a Supreme Intelligence or Will gives direction to the Universe and to things in the Universe. Other kinds of order in the teleological argument do not necessarily entail this kind of directional activity. This directional activity requires an Intelligence or Will.

But can we rightly say that intelligence or will is a *cause* giving direction to our activity? The answer can be "yes" in one respect and it can be "no" in another. Our intelligence and will can be seen to be very much involved as causal factors in putting wood, cement, sand, and water together to build a house. We also can say that without the presence of intelligence and will, that house would not have come into existence. Now of course intelligence and will do not *create* the matter which they use to build the house but rearrange already existing matter into different types of material to be used in different ways and for different purposes. In this sense we cannot call intelligence and will "Absolute" causes, or causes that create *ex nihilo.*

Intelligence and will do not originate or create energy or force, but they can be said to be the applications of very specific kinds of energies and forces. Let us assume that intelligence and will can start things going. They can originate a series of directional activities toward some goal or purpose. I "will" to move my arm and body. I intelligently perceive the long-term steps that have to be taken to get things moving and changed. Again I am not creating energy that was not there before in some way. Energy is being focused and manifested differently. There are billions of complex neurological patterns and biochemical changes going on at each act of intelligence and will. Forms of energy are being constantly changed into other forms of energy in an interaction of structures of the body with its environment. Intelligence and will do not create this energy or the interplay of changing forms of energy. The most we can say is that intelligence and will are some of the forms of energy being manifested—and of course to us a very important form.

Thus some form of energy (function of neurons) is *prior* to intelligence and will, and intelligence and will are forms of energy being expressed in the Universe. (They perhaps can be seen as one of the thousands of forms and manifestations of energy that we try to explain by subsuming them under general laws or explanations.) Order, regularity, and design are brought about by many different kinds of natural events and forces acting in many different ways. Directional activity found in natural objects is one very prominent kind. Intelligence and will is another. The directional activity produced by intelligence and will is another. Intelligence is one of the many events in the Universe. Intelligence is one of the many things in the Universe producing design and order and directional activity. It is too great a jump to say that the Universe itself has a Supreme Intelligence to account for all directional activity whether it be natural such as in the acorn, or due to human intelligence and will such as in building a house. Intelligence and will are ingredients *in* the Universe. They are products *of* a Universe, but not *characteristics* of the Universe itself.

7.8   Are There Other Alternatives for Explaining Design? Accident, Chance, Evolution. The teleological argument in general, and Aquinas' version of it in particular, assume that the purposive, directional activity of inanimate things cannot be explained by chance, by accident, by randomness, or by fortuitous circumstances. Their activity must be, and can only be, explained in terms of an Intelligence operating to determine and guide them to their goals. Neither chance nor accident can explain the existence of goal-directed design in nature. Chance cannot do it, therefore intelligence does. Whenever we see activity that is erratic, unpredictable, irregular, unexplainable, or accidental, we attribute that activity to chance. Whenever we see activity that is predictable, regular, explainable, nonerratic, nonaccidental, we attribute that activity to an operating intelligence.

But is it not possible to have activity which is predictable, regular, and explainable and *not* attribute it to an operating intelligence? We can and *do* have explanations of purposive or directional activity of inanimate things without reference to any intelligence planning or directing the activty. We do explain the function and purpose of the heart, of our liver, of our eyes without reference to an intelligence making these functions possible. Is chance the only alternative to intelligence? Perhaps chance is a name for our ignorance of the causal conditions operating without intention. Is luck another alternative? Is accident another alternative? Is natural law another alternative? There are many ways by which things come to be the way they are and do what they do.

One cannot talk meaningfully about the Universe having come into being by Accident or by Chance. Some order or other has existed in the Universe eternally. To say that the Universe came into being by Accident implies a contrast with something planned to come into being but which plan did not work out. To say that the Universe happened by Chance is to personify Chance as one does Luck and treat it as a causal entity, which it is not. If the Universe is eternal, Blind Chance need not be referred to as an explanation for the Universe itself. Things in the Universe may be labelled as happening by accident or chance.

They would thus mainly refer to that distribution and retransformation of the energy in the Universe which is not directed by any intelligent planning or foresight. They thus do not exclude lawful relationships or analysis. Accident and chance are not lawless.

Assessment of the argument. The first weakness in this argument is the assumption that highly organized results, even those occurring in a pattern involving a goal state, must be due to a plan. They may in fact be due to the operation of either natural laws or chance, or both. The extraordinary coincidence between the positioning of stalactites and stalagmites in the great limestone caverns, such that there is always one directly below the other, is not due to chance nor to a plan; it is due to the fact that the lower one is formed by the water dripping off the upper one. The remarkable distribution of numbers in the results from an unbiased roulette wheel, such that there is a closer and closer approximation to the same proportion of each possibility the longer this random machine operates, is purely due to chance; indeed it is the very evidence that only chance is operating. The interlocking patterns in the world of living creatures are simply the result of the laws of natural selection operating on the random mutations of genes; chance produces the initial variation, and natural selection, i.e., their suitability to their environment, determines whether they stay around long enough to reproduce or reproduce more effectively than the other forms then present. Consequently, the forms that do survive exhibit considerable suitability for their environment. The argument from "design" is simply a fallacious argument from *functional order* to a *designer;* it is fallacious because there is a much better explanation of the order, namely, the operation of evolution. This is a much better explanation because it involves only claims that can easily be supported by evidence and follows immediately from these claims. We can even demonstrate the evolutionary process in a laboratory, controlling its rate and modifying the direction it takes by manipulating the conditions (energy supply, population density, mutation rate, etc.) At this stage in the history of science it seems entirely clear that this *is* the explanation. Hence, introducing any new and hitherto-unknown entities such as a supernatural planner is entirely indefensible.

The steps in the evolution of inorganic chemicals into organisms are now as unmysterious as the steps in the evolution of man from simple organisms, and we may refer to the combination of both processes as the evolution of man from nonlife. The first of these steps is perhaps the most important for the teleological argument since it bridges the gap from the clearly non-purposive to the clearly purposive. For those unfamiliar with the research, the basic process is the shuffling around of inorganic ions in water, with the action of wind, evaporation, and lightning discharges, which eventually results in their linking up end to end into long-chain organic molecules; these then act as templates to which similar ions attach themselves laterally until a second chain forms alongside the first, from which it is separated by physical or electrical shock, giving the beginning of the reproductive process. And now the competition for survival of various organic compounds formed in this way begins, in terms of their relative stability, speed of formation in the "soup," etc.; eventually some of these systems build up some internal articulation, component coordination, and transformational feeding—and life is on its way.

The supporter of the teleological argument does not usually give up at this point. He will say that we have merely pushed the difficulty one stage further back. The question now becomes, Why are the *laws of nature* and the *properties of matter* such as to produce the remarkable patterning that we observe? The argument does not assert that the Planner intervenes at the last step in the process of planning, only that the order in the final product requires that there be a planner somewhere. Behind the superficially random operation of the roulette wheel, there is actually the operation of other laws of nature and application we are not aware at the time we spin the wheel. Our ignorance leads us to call the result random, but fundamentally this process, too, is one exhibiting design. If we achieved an historically complete account of contemporary order, carrying it back to an originally existing mass of plasma (or whatever it was, if it was), the question becomes, Where did *that* material get *its* special properties, such that the intelligent activity and coordinated properties of contemporary things were able to evolve from them? And if the Universe had no beginning, the question still arises about the particular laws that it obeys.

This move is not simply an extension of the original point but a shift to quite a different and wholly dubious arena for the argument. For at first we asked for an explanation of certain effects in the world of nature which are clearly present. And such explanations are commonly given—as they can be in this case—by appealing to the nature of the entities involved and the laws governing their behavior. We can even explain some of these laws and properties in terms of other laws and properties. But the request to explain the ultimate laws and properties, or *all* the laws and properties *together*, is just like the misguided request to explain the existence of the first material state or of an infinite totality of states (which we discussed in connection with the cosmological argument).[10]

10. From *Primary Philosophy* by Michael Scriven, pp. 126–28. Copyright 1966 by McGraw-Hill Book Company. Used with permission of McGraw-Hill Book Company.

The best example of purposiveness and "directional" activity has been thought to be the process of evolution. Can the evolution of species be explained other than with reference to a Designer or Supreme Intelligence? Darwin's theory of natural selection (struggle for survival; survival of the fittest; variation; hereditary transmission of genetic material; adaptation) attempts to give such an explanation.

> . . .In order to pass the B.A. examination, it was, also, necessary to get up Paley's *Evidences of Christianity,* and his *Moral Philosophy.* This was done in a thorough manner, and I am convinced that I could have written out the whole of the *Evidences* with perfect correctness, but not of course in the clear language of Paley.The logic of this book and as I may add of his *Natural Theology* gave me as much delight as did Euclid. The careful study of these works, without attempting to learn any part by rote, was the only part of the Academical Course which, as I then felt and as I still believe, was of the least use to me in the education of my mind. I did not at that time trouble myself about Paley's premises; and taking these on trust I was charmed and convinced by the long line of argumentation. By answering well the examination questions in Paley, by doing Euclid well, and by not failing miserably in Classics, I gained a good place among the οἱ πολλοί, or crowd of men who do not go in for honours.[11]

> During these two years (October 1836 to January 1839) I was led to think much about religion. Whilst on board the *Beagle* I was quite orthodox, and I remember being heartily laughed at by several of the officers (though themselves orthodox) for quoting the Bible as an unanswerable authority on some point of morality. I suppose it was the novelty of the argument that amused them. But I had gradually come, by this time, to see that the Old Testament from its manifestly false history of the world, with the Tower of Babel, the rainbow as a sign, etc., etc., and from its attributing to God the feelings of a revengeful tyrant, was no more to be trusted than the sacred books of the Hindoos, or the beliefs of any barbarian. The question then continually rose before my mind and would not be banished,—is it credible that if God were now to make a revelation to the Hindoos, would he permit it to be connected with the belief in Vishnu, Siva, &c., as Christianity is connected with the Old Testament. This appeared to me utterly incredible.

> By further reflecting that the clearest evidence would be requisite to make any sane man believe in the miracles by which Christianity is supported,—that the more we know of the fixed laws of nature

---

11. Nora Barlow, ed., *The Autobiography of Charles Darwin 1809–1882* (London: Collins, 1958), p. 59. Reprinted by permission of A. D. Peters and Company.

the more incredible do miracles become,—that the men at that time were ignorant and credulous to a degree almost incomprehensible by us,—that the Gospels cannot be proved to have been written simultaneously with the events,—that they differ in many important details, far too important as it seemed to me to be admitted as the usual inaccuracies of eyewitnesses;—by such reflections as these, which I give not as having the least novelty or value, but as they influenced me, I gradually came to disbelieve in Christianity as a divine revelation. The fact that many false religions have spread over large portions of the earth like wild-fire had some weight with me. Beautiful as is the morality of the New Testament, it can hardly be denied that its perfection depends in part on the interpretation which we now put on metaphors and allegories. . . .

. . .The old argument of design in nature, as given by Paley, which formerly seemed to me so conclusive, fails, now that the law of natural selection has been discovered. We can no longer argue that, for instance, the beautiful hinge of a bivalve shell must have been made by an intelligent being, like the hinge of a door by man. There seems to be no more design in the variability of organic beings and in the action of natural selection, than in the course which the wind blows.[12]

That there is much suffering in the world no one disputes. Some have attempted to explain this in reference to man by imagining that it serves for his moral improvement. But the number of men in the world is as nothing compared with that of all other sentient beings, and these often suffer greatly without any moral improvement. A being so powerful and so full of knowledge as a God who could create the universe, is to our finite minds omnipotent and omniscient, and it revolts our understanding to suppose that his benevolence is not unbounded, for what advantage can there be in the sufferings of millions of the lower animals throughout almost endless time? This very old argument from the existence of suffering against the existence of an intelligent first cause seems to me a strong one; whereas, as just remarked, the presence of much suffering agrees well with the view that all organic beings have been developed through variation and natural selection.

At the present day the most usual argument for the existence of an intelligent God is drawn from the deep inward conviction and feelings which are experienced by most persons. But it cannot be doubted that Hindoos, Mahomadans and others might argue in the same manner and with equal force in favour of the existence of one God, or of many Gods, or as with the Buddists of no God. There are also many barbarian tribes who cannot be said with any

---

12. Ibid., pp. 85–87.

truth to believe in what we call God: they believe indeed in spirits or ghosts, and it can be explained, as Tyler and Herbert Spencer have shown, how such a belief would be likely to arise.[13]

How do you explain the existence of the long necks of giraffes? The camouflage of lizards? The sharp teeth and claws and sharp sense of smell of a leopard? The swiftness of an antelope? The warm fur and the hibernation of a bear? The changes of the eye over a period of millions of years to produce vision? The instinct of bees and ants? These are some of the kinds of "design" that natural selection attempts to explain without reference to a Designer. The attempt to explain the existence of organisms and of man without recourse to a Supranatural Being has its roots in ancient Greece as far back as Anaximander (611–547 B.C.) who was a student of Thales, the founder of western philosophy and science.

> 2.30 He held that the first animals arose in moisture, being enclosed in spiny "barks", but that as they grew older they emerged onto the drier land and there (the "bark" having ruptured) lived a different sort of life for a short time.

> 2.31 He says further that in the beginning man was born from animals of a different sort, arguing from the fact that whereas animals are soon able to fend for themselves, the young of humans are dependent for a long period of time. Hence, if man had been in the beginning as he is now, he would never have been able to survive.[14]

It was not until Charles Darwin's time that evolutionary theories based upon paleontological, geological, and geographical evidence were developed. With the publication in 1859 of the *Origin of Species* the theory of natural selection became an alternative hypothesis for explaining design in organic life as opposed to attributing it to a Designer. Organisms gradually evolve over a long period of time from simple structures such as amoebas to the most complex structures such as the primates and man. In this process those organisms will survive that can survive, or that have the structures to survive in a constant struggle of organisms with each other and with their environment. They must adapt to survive. This does not mean they must always keep changing their structures. Ants have existed very much as they are now for over seventy-five million

13. Ibid., pp. 90–91.

14. From *An Introduction to Early Greek Philosophy*, by John Manley Robinson, p. 33. Houghton Mifflin Company, 1968. Reprinted by permission of the publishers. The first quotation is from Aetius and the second from Plutarch.

years. But if the organism's structures do not facilitate adaptation then they must change or the organism will cease to exist in its struggle for existence. Those that have survived are able to transmit their changes through heredity, through procreation. Some of these changes are due to mutations. Variation of species is one of the results of mutation. These mutations are random, accidental, nonintentional, and spontaneous. (There are cases of humans producing guided and directed mutations, for example in strains of pneumococcus, where the results were somewhat predictable due to the controlled situation. Here intelligence *is* doing the directing.)

Giraffes existed at one time in quite a different form from their present one. There may have been a period of time when giraffes with short necks could not reach the tops of trees to gather food during periods of drought and climatic changes. Those with short necks died off more rapidly. Those with longer necks tended to survive. From generation to generation hereditary characteristics were being passed on. The genetic trait for "long-neckedness" persisted and won out because it helped the organism survive. It can now be seen to be the most general adaptive feature of a giraffe. This kind of adaptive process measured in terms of our years is a long one and has been going on for over fifteen billion years from the first formation of amino acids into proteins and cells to the present day. An increase in complexity and in variety and an increase in *novel functions* characterizes the evolutionary process.

A common criticism of natural selection is that it may explain the survival of the species but not the *arrival*. We must postulate a God who assists in the arrival of species. But the mechanism by which an organism has survived *is* the explanation of its arrival. Survival is arrival.

Is there a general direction and a progressive movement to evolution that cannot be accounted for except in terms of a Supreme Intelligence or Designer? When you compare man to a one-celled animal there does seem to be an advance. (Or should we say only a difference?) Man is more complex. His behavior is much more variable. He is more adaptive. He has intelligence, language, social structures, cultures, bombs. But there are instances where an amoeba can adapt and we cannot. There are occasions where more complexity and variability are a hindrance rather than an advantage for survival—where intelligence used incorrectly may be a detriment rather than an asset for continued existence. Thus saying that evolution is an advance depends on the criteria by which one judges the matter. Is that criterion survival? The existence of consciousness? It also depends on how long a time span one looks at. Some dinosaurs existed for over 50 million years, some oysters for over 200 million years. We have been around about 1 million 500,000 years. Looked at from a long enough time span, say a few thousand billion years, would there be an advance or a direction to the process? Looking at 2 million years, we can see shifts, blind alleys, reversals of what we regard as the advance or direction. But even if we could establish objectively a general drift to evolution toward an advance this would not entail a Designer or an Intelligence directing this process. It would be an indication that within the Universe there are evolutionary processes, this being one of them, which have tendencies toward advance or progress, and perhaps there are tendencies in the Universe toward the annihilation and/or containment of progressive advance.

It is not evident that evolution has taken place in an orderly manner in the sense in which "orderly" is meant, that is, the continuous protracted application of Forethought by a Supreme Intelligence to bring about a chain of events culminating in increase in complexity and in the development of man. Our phrases about evolution such as "evolutionary process," "in the course of evolution," "evolutionary progress," even "natural selection" tend to make us picture evolution as if it were a well-unified process, a monistic course intentioned and guided by some Being. We can, looking back over the process, picture it as unified, as interrelated, and as monistic as we wish but that may be a product of the refinements of our ability to abstract and our ability to isolate universal features by ignoring what we consider as incidental, unimportant, and as the exception. But even to say that there is an Order that is fairly Monistic is not to have to accept the conclusion that there is a Mind or Orderer as its source. Also to say that a Monistic Order is not due to an Orderer is not to be involved in contradiction.

VIII

God as All-Good and Omnipotent: The Problem of Evil

8.1 Evolution and the Problem of an All-Good Designer. We have seen that evolution can be explained without reference to a Designer. We also have suggested that a creature's *survival* is its *arrival* and we need not argue that God uses natural selection as His method of arriving at Greater Complexity, or at Perfection, or at Man, or at the Fulfillment of His Purpose for the Universe.

But let us go into the problem a little further and see what additional difficulties we may encounter. Does Evolution support the existence of a Good Design (The Best of all Possible Worlds) and/or the existence of an All-Good Designer? A Benevolent Designer would be one that was morally and compassionately concerned about the creatures that He has Created.

> . . .the belief in a benevolent designer, one who cared about his creatures and did not wish them to suffer, has always been the mainspring of belief in design. People would not be so likely to be attracted to the argument from design if they thought that the cosmic designer was malevolent. Yet it was precisely the belief in a benevolent designer that was difficult to sustain in the face of the belief in the evolutionary process, for the evolutionary process is a scene of continuous and endless strife, pain, and death. Life is a struggle for existence, in which many species die out and every individual inevitably dies—most often in direct agony, through

starvation, cold, disease, or being eaten alive by other animals. The individual life is expendable: millions of individuals of every species die every day (usually before they have lived out a full life), but life continues through their offspring, who in their turn die in pain and suffering. Does the designer inflict all this suffering merely to preserve the species, at the expense of the individual; and of what value is a species if all the individuals in it must live a life of constant threat and insecurity and finally die in pain and suffering? Besides, nature is no more careful of the species or type than of the individual: thousands of species have perished through starvation, changes in climate, being attacked by other animals, or because some new mutation arose that was swifter or more adaptable. Nature throughout is red with blood.[1]

There is much pain and suffering, both physical and mental, that is accidental, irrelevant, purposeless, capricious, wanton, and unnecessary. Pain serves a useful function in evolution as a sign of danger, disease, or damage. But even in evolution and in man's civilization pain has too often gone beyond any useful function as a warning. Sometimes it serves no useful function. Sometimes there is more pain than is required to indicate that something has gone wrong. Some pain continues even after it performs its function as a stimulus. Sometimes in the act of dying there is unendurable pain. It is difficult for many to comprehend how an Omnipotent God and an All-Loving God could allow so much agony and grief in Nature.

There is much waste of good potential in life. There are the incurably sick and deformed, the injured, the diseased and maimed, the mentally retarded and physically handicapped. These conditions are caused independently of the desires, wishes, and will of the organism. Then there are the people who have everything—not much pain in life, a lot of fame, quickness of intelligence, beauty, health, position, and healthy old age. There are those who suffer undeservedly; infant children unmercifully battered by parents; the innocents of the world condemned to agony by war, political power, and oppression. Why are pain and suffering distributed so unfairly? There is much in existence that is incongruent with a Designer who is Kind, Loving, Caring, and Good.

The teleological argument always chooses instances of design which are useful, functional, beautiful, good, valuable, noble, and advantageous to human beings. The existence of vision, the patterns of the seasons bringing with them growth and fertility, the combination of protein molecules to produce life, the intricate coordination of millions of neural

---

1. John Hospers, *An Introduction to Philosophical Analysis*, 2d ed. © 1967, p. 458. Reprinted by permission of Prentice-Hall, Inc., Englewood Cliffs, New Jersey.

changes to cause thought. The teleological argument does not select instances of design, or proofs of design, which are dysfunctional, or dysteleological. There are things which are ignoble, ugly, painful, bad, disadvantageous. The existence of cataracts on the eye, the patterns of the seasons bringing with them death and barrenness, the combinations of changes producing syphillis and cancer, the intricate coordination of millions of neural changes to cause hysteria and schizophrenia. These events exist and are as complex as the ones the teleological argument chooses to present.

Why does the teleological argument choose only examples which are valuable and beneficial to man? The answer is to be found in a form of anthropomorphism and/or theocentricism. If we were God then we would desire and work to produce these valuable things. (Fortunately for us God-concepts were not constructed by sadists, although there are sadistic elements in some of the God-concepts which religions have held.) The answer is also to be found in assuming that because there are good things for us in existence they then must be produced by a God who has a virtuous nature similar to our own. In a major sense these answers commit a fallacy. They say that a virtuous mind such as man's produces good things, therefore good things are produced by a virtuous mind. This is applied in an analogy to God. It does not follow that just because a virtuous mind produces good things we then can reverse it and say that good things are produced by a virtuous mind. Good things might very well be produced in other ways, such as by natural events.

If the teleological argument uses the good in the world as evidence of a Good God, then we could without inconsistency use Evil in the world as evidence of an Evil God. Generally though this is not done. It is done in Zoroastrianism which was the religion of Persia before it became Moslem. Its prophet Zoroaster (or Zarathustra) and its sacred text the *Zend-Avesta* teaches that Ormazd is the Lord of Light and of Good. He battles against Ahriman and all his evil hosts. Ormazd created man to help him win against Ahriman. The ultimate Good Kingdom will be fulfilled. This belief is found in the Christian concept of Satan (for example in Christian Manichaeanism and in Milton's *Paradise Lost*.) In Christianity though the battle is a hoax. God *created* Satan as his leading Angel. Satan became rebellious and tried to take over and God banished Him. Satan has ceaselessly continued to undo God's good work. God could, if He wanted to, overthrow Satan at any moment. Satan is not All-Powerful. (Why doesn't God destroy Satan once and for all? Does He enjoy having His work thwarted so often?) In the End God will win out and the Kingdom of Good will reign supreme. In some interpretations that Kingdom will come with the help of man, and in other interpretations without the help of man. Man has a choice to join or not to join in the battle. (Every religion sees the End as the Kingdom of Good with the Kingdom of Evil losing out. Also no religion holds that the Good God was Created out of the Darkness of an Evil God who existed eternally.)

In the teleological argument from design God is characterized as The Most Intelligent, The Most Powerful, and The Most Benevolent Designer. He therefore must display his Goodness by choosing loving and compassionate means to arrive at His ends. Is God's purpose the happiness, comfort, and convenience of man and all animals or is God's purpose to try our souls and to force us to seek salvation? How are we to explain the presence of evil, pain, and suffering on the assumption that God is All-Good, All Powerful, All-Knowing and Completely Perfect?

8.2   God as Completely Perfect, Omnipotent, Omniscient, Omnibenevolent and the Problem of Evil. We shall discuss the Problem of Evil in the context of a God who concerns himself with man. Man's plight is of importance to God as a son's plight is to a loving father. The traditional Problem of Evil stems from assuming three things, only two of which are compatible.

(1) God is Omnibenevolent.

(2) God is Omnipotent.

(3) Evil exists.

The ancient Greek philosopher Epicurus (342–270 B.C.) posed the problem in this way, to those who believed in a God who had those first two characteristics:

Is God willing to prevent Evil, but is not able to prevent Evil?

Then He is not Omnipotent.

Is God able to prevent Evil but not willing to prevent Evil?

Then He is Malevolent.

Is God both able to prevent Evil *and* willing to prevent Evil?

Then where does Evil come from?

We find David Hume also presenting the same problem:

If the Evil in the World is from the intention of the Deity, then He is not Benevolent.

If the Evil in the World is contrary to His intention, then He is not Omnipotent.

But it is either in accordance with His intention or contrary to it.

Therefore, either the Deity is not Benevolent or He is not Omnipotent.

Thus we see that the three statements taken together are incompatible:

If (1) and (2) then not (3).
If (2) and (3) then not (1).
If (3) and (1) then not (2).

If God is Omnibenevolent (1) and Omnipotent (2), then there is no Evil (3)—or there should not be any Evil (3).

If God is Omnipotent (2) and Evil (3) exists, then God cannot be Omnibenevolent (1).

If Evil (3) exists and God is Omnibenevolent (1), then God cannot be Omnipotent (2).

Another way of putting this is: God is both All-Good and All-Powerful. Evil exists. Either God causes that Evil (or permits that Evil) or God does not. Therefore God is either not All-Good or not All-Powerful. That is, He cannot be both All-Good and All-Powerful.

We tend to want to relieve God of responsibility for the existence of any Evil in the Universe. Can we? The problem is further aggravated when we add the traditional quality Omniscience (All-Knowing). God knows all things that have happened, are happening, and will happen.

A man can be excused sometimes for doing the wrong thing or failing to do the right thing. He can be absolved of responsibility. He was ignorant of the law of the country he was in and drove on the wrong side of the street. Or he had a lapse of memory and before he knew it ended up driving on the wrong side of the street and running over a child. Man can be excused or blamed for doing evil things on the basis of his uncontrolled temper, his lack of motivation, his overweening pride or aggressiveness, his being provoked, his selfishness and egocentricity, his prudishness, his greed and voluptuousness. Can an All-Good God and an Omnipotent God be similarly excused?

If Omniscience is added to the characteristic of God we then have

the problem in another perspective. The child was walking across the
street to a birthday party at the time of the accident. The injured child
was rushed to the hospital by the driver and the child died on arrival.
An Omniscient God would know all this. An Omnipotent God would
presumably allow this to happen since He could with His Omnipotence
prevent it. But an Omnibenevolent God would certainly not like, or
value, or want this sort of thing to happen.

Now let us add the characteristic "Completely Perfect." If God is Completely Perfect then His Will must be Perfect. What He Wills must
be compatible with his Perfect Nature. If existence is not Perfect then
this is an indication that His Will is not Perfect and His Nature is not
Completely Perfect. Does this mean that He is not Omnipotent since
if He were He could have Created Himself to be a Completely Perfect
Being? Or does it mean that He lacks Self-Love and thus is not quite
Omnibenevolent at least to Himself? This lack itself would prevent Him
from being Completely Perfect. Let us proceed now from the statement
of the Problem of Evil to the attempted solutions.

8.3 This Is the Best of All Possible Worlds. "Theodicy" is the
name given to the discipline which attempts to justify the ways of God
to man, or in Leibniz's sense to defend the belief that this is the Best
of All Possible Worlds. God is All-Powerful. God is All-Good and Evil
does exist. The three are compatible when seen in the light of the
contention that anything other than what Exists would have been worse.
Any other Universe would have more Evil in it than the present one.
(This implies further beliefs which we will examine later, such as, that
all Evil is Necessary and Unavoidable in order to have the Best of All
Possible Worlds.) Any Universe necessarily entails some Evil if it is
to be guided by Laws. One last implication which must be made explicit
is that all the Evil in this Universe which is the Best of All Possible
Ones is much less in amount than the Good.

If God is Completely Perfect and Omniscient He would be conscious
of all the possible alternatives and would will the preferred alternatives
in the light of His Perfection and Goodness. God Desires and wills the
Best Possible every time He chooses. God also would be aware of the
consequences of any and all alternatives which were *not* taken. This
view is based on the assumption which is presupposed by the teleological
argument that things happen in the best possible way.

Are we able on any ground to say that this is the Best of All Possible
Worlds? Is this the kind of world we would have created if we were
such a God? Would we not have created a world with no evil, or with
much less evil than is present in it? If we had the power and the

knowledge and the goodness we would have created this world differently from what it is. This does not seem to be the sort of world an All-Good God would have created if He were Omnipotent. At times we feel that this is not such a bad world. We do not usually feel that this is the worst of all possible worlds. But in spite of these feelings we often do believe that this world could be better than it is or that surely the world could have less evil in it and in that sense things would be better. Also there do seem to be evils that could have been avoided and that are unnecessary (diseases, earthquakes, floods, pestilence, famine, cancer). Could it be that God in fact is *preventing* the Best of All Possible Worlds by holding back? Could it be that God creates the World for Himself, and the World is the Best of All Possible Worlds for Him, but not for us?

8.4 *Evil Does Not Exist, Evil Is an Illusion.* If evil does not exist, then we do not have the Problem of Evil. We then have the problem of how someone can argue that there is no evil in the world. Human beings disagree on what evil is but most human beings do regard some things as evil and some things as good. Human beings normally consider excessive pain, suffering, infliction of cruelty upon helpless children as evil and try to remedy such situations. These things are part of our world and they do in fact exist.

If we say that Evil is an illusion we cannot then say that evil does not exist. That "illusion" certainly has an existence all its own. Some pain and suffering are illusory but even such illusory pain can be painful and real and evil. It is not any better that the pain is an illusion. Sometimes it is worse because it is an illusion. If what we feel and see as evil is not real evil but an illusion, or deficiency of our understanding, or ability to control our mind, then such illusions and deficiencies in themselves are evil and indicate a lack of Goodness and Perfection in the Designer. A world without such crucial mistakes would be a better world.

This explanation of evil is inconsistent with one of the most common ingredients of all religions, namely that some things in the world are evil or sinful and that not all evil is illusory or nonexistent. We can relate this point to the previous section 8.3 in this way: Everything except God is, and must be kept, finite, limited, less good, and imperfect. Everything except God must contain evil to some extent. Evil of some sort must exist. For God to have created another Completely Perfect Being would mean that He would have had to create another thing like Himself—an identical thing without any evil at all. Obviously He did not and does not want to do this even though it is not logically impossible for God to do. In fact, He could have created many such Beings, or at least one other one.

8.5 *Evil Is the Privation of Good.* Augustine in his *City of God* and other works tries to show that evil is a *lack* of a good, or a *negation* of the good, or the *privation* of a good. This was the Neo-Platonic attempt in Christianity to de-emphasize the importance and presence of evil in the world in order to bolster the Goodness of God. Evil was a cause that was deficient or incomplete. Since all these things were in major respects regarded as "nonbeings" (as being causally ineffective), and "nonbeing" cannot exist (for if it did exist it would not be nonbeing), then evil does not exist. Evil has no substantive existence.

Evil may be a lack of a good, or the negation, or the privation, or the incompleted state of a good, but why should such lacks, negations, privations, incompleted states exist in a world governed by an All-Powerful and all-Good God? We can say that blindness is a lack of sight, or the privation of vision, or an incompleted state of seeing, but nevertheless blindness is a handicap. One may call leukemia a nonbeing, or privation, or absence of healthy cells, but why is there this absence of healthy cells if the Universe is governed by an Omnipotent and Omnibenevolent God? Why should there be goods that are missing, or corrupted, or negated? If God is All-Powerful and All-Good and He is responsible for the existing good in the world, then He also must be responsible for any absence of good.

> It may console the paralytic to be told that paralysis is mere lack of mobility, nothing positive, and that insofar as he *is*, he is perfect. It is not clear, however, that this kind of comfort is available to the sufferer from malaria. He will reply that his trouble is not that he lacks anything, but rather that he has too much of something, namely, protozoans of the genus *Plasmodium*. If the theist retorts that evil is nonbeing in the metaphysical, not the crudely material, sense, it would seem appropriate for the victim to inquire why God saw fit that the finitude of His creatures should take just this form rather than some other. Really, the "evil is nonbeing" ploy is a play on words, an unfunny joke. It is a sign of progress both in philosophical acumen and essential humanness, that little is heard along these lines nowadays.[2]

The belief that evil and pain are not anything positive but are negative, that they are merely privations of a Good, seems hardly satisfactory

2. Reprinted from Wallace I. Matson: *The Existence of God.* Copyright © 1965 by Cornell University, pp. 142–43. Used by permission of Cornell University Press.

and not at all compatible with the very existing pain and evil that men feel and undergo and want to eradicate.

8.6 God's Goodness Is Not Our Kind of Goodness; The Ways of God Are Not the Ways of Man. How do we know God's Goodness is not our kind of goodness? It is impossible to argue that God's Goodness is far different from our notion of goodness if we do not know something about God's Goodness. In what sense can it be said that God's Goodness is not our kind of goodness? Are God's standards for judging good different from ours? If this amounts to our saying that God cannot be considered good in any of our senses of the term, then we are left with wondering what sense the term could have with reference to God. We can only talk about God's Good in our sense of good and if this is taken away then there can be no relevance to the word.

> Here, then, I take my stand on the acknowledged principle of logic and of morality, that when we mean different things we have no right to call them by the same name, and to apply to them the same predicates, moral and intellectual. Language has no meaning for the words Just, Merciful, Benevolent, save that in which we predicate them of our fellow-creatures; and unless that is what we intend to express by them, we have no business to employ the words. If in affirming them of God we do not mean to affirm these very qualities, differing only as greater in degree, we are neither philosophically nor morally entitled to affirm them at all. If it be said that the qualities are the same, but that we cannot conceive them as they are when raised to the infinite, I grant that we cannot adequately conceive them in one of their elements, their infinity. But we can conceive them in their other elements, which are the very same in the infinite as in the finite development. Anything carried to the infinite must have all the properties of the same thing as finite, except those which depend upon the finiteness.

> . . .What belongs to it either as Infinite or as Absolute I do not pretend to know; but I know that infinite goodness must be goodness, and that what is not consistent with goodness, is not consistent with infinite goodness. If in ascribing goodness to God I do not mean what I mean by goodness; if I do not mean the goodness of which I have some knowledge, but an incomprehensible attribute of an incomprehensible substance, which for aught I know may be a totally different quality from that which I love and venerate . . . what do I mean by calling it goodness? And what reason have I for venerating it? If I know nothing about what the attribute is, I cannot tell that it is a proper object of veneration. To say that God's goodness may be different in kind from man's goodness,

what is it but saying, with a slight change of phraseology, that God may possibly not be good? To assert in words what we do not think in meaning, is as suitable a definition as can be given of a moral falsehood. Besides, suppose that certain unknown attributes are ascribed to the Deity in a religion the external evidences of which are so conclusive to my mind, as effectually to convince me that it comes from God. Unless I believe God to possess the same moral attributes which I find, in however inferior a degree, in a good man, what ground of assurance have I of God's veracity?

. . . But when I am told that I must believe this, and at the same time call this being by the names which express and affirm the highest human morality, I say in plain terms that I will not. Whatever power such a being may have over me, there is one thing which he shall not do; he shall not compel me to worship him. I will call no being good, who is not what I mean when I apply that epithet to my fellow-creatures; and if such a being can sentence me to hell for not so calling him, to hell I will go.[3]

If God's concept of Good is of a different kind than ours, if His Ways are not our ways, then His judgment of good and evil would be quite different from ours. How could we make a moral judgment about God and about His Ways? Would we perhaps find God doing and advocating things which were not good at all in our sense of the word? Would we then have to judge things as good and bad to us in terms of our attitudes and feelings in contra-distinction to God's Goodness? If God exists in the traditional sense then we were created to know His Good, and our good. He created us in such a way so as to enable us to perceive what is good or at least to develop the abilities to find out. God is obligated in this way. If God did not do these things for us then He would be less than All-Good. He would have committed an error. He would have omitted something very important and necessary in assisting man to get closer to God through a moral life akin to His Wishes. The definitions of man's good are often expressed in terms of God's Will and God's Goodness. If we have no conception of His Goodness then how do we know how to do God's Will? How are we to follow God's Commands?

When we argue that we have no right to judge God's Ways, or what is Good or Evil with reference to God because we are finite creatures and cannot really know Him, we then are involved in judging according to a double standard. We judge the moral behavior of a man on one

---

3. John Stuart Mill, *An Examination of Sir William Hamilton's Philosophy* (London: Logmans, Green, Reader and Dyer, 1878), pp. 127–29.

level (for example his using painful means to arrive at an end when less painful means were available for him to use), but then judge God's behavior by other more excusing standards in order to defend the "good" characteristics of our God. Or we avoid the problem by refusing to apply any standard of judgment upon God at all, calling it all inscrutable. If in our finiteness we can never know the inscrutable Ways of God, if Evil in the World must always remain a mystery to us, then what are we to say when our finiteness tells us about the other characteristics of God such as Omnipotence, Omniscience, Omnipresence? They describe God and depict a knowledge of Him. Arguing in this way that God is a mystery and His Ways are inscrutable prevents us from saying that God is Good, or not-Good. It also prevents us from saying tha God's Goodness is not our kind of goodness for how would we know?

8.7 Evil Exists in Order to Build Character; Evil Is a Test of Man; Good Comes Out of Evil. God could have created every'.ning perfect for everyone. (We will see in the section on free will a.id evil that God did just that with the Garden of Eden.) There would have been no diseases or excessive pain; no problems and anxieties; no cruelty; no guilt; no major shortcomings. We would have had all the food we wanted whenever we wanted it; easy transportation to other parts of the Universe; comfortable and quick ways of learning; beautiful relations with other people and with oneself. But had God done this, He would have spoiled us. (Although if God is Omnipotent then He could have made things so that even with these goods, self-indulgent, unappreciative, insensitive human beings lacking self-initiative would *not* have been produced.) Had God created a Perfect World without evil, without anyone having any obstacles to overcome, then man would never have the opportunity to express and acquire such qualities as sensitivity, intelligence, hope, faith, compassion, charity, initiative, perseverance, and choice. Man would not be a moral creature, and moral virtues would not exist. The existence of moral virtues in a man is a good; they ought to exist in the Universe. They must exist, and God has seen to it that they do. God brings these qualities and virtues into existence in the only possible way that they can be brought into existence, by allowing evil to exist. (Pain and suffering may serve as an opportunity for man to be moral and virtuous, but this argument cannot be used to apply to the pain and suffering in the animal kingdom.)

It is a truism and rather trivial to say that some evil in the world has to exist otherwise man would have no challenges. But it does not follow that man can only develop and grow in intelligence and in emotional maturity by means of the presence of evil, suffering, and pain.

It does not necessarily follow that man can develop and grow in intelligence and in emotional maturity only with the present amount of evil in the world. Less would have sufficed if it is true that evil has any effect at all. An Omnipotent God could have created less and still have achieved the result. Man's intelligence and maturity do develop in the context of struggle against obstacles. Sometimes this struggle suppresses growth; sometimes pain, struggle, and suffering cause people to be less human. These things depend on the personalities involved, on the amount and kind of struggle, and on the sense of helplessness or hopefulness.

This approach to the Problem of Evil holds that God puts obstacles in man's way in order to have man develop his character and intelligence. We again see a confusion of an "effect" with an "end intended." The existence of Evil may indeed on many occasions produce intelligent responses and emotional development, but from this descriptive fact we cannot claim that evil is purposely put there by God for this reason. Certainly Helen Keller did overcome many crises and problems which to most people would be insurmountable, and certainly her fine character was formed out of such a struggle. But it is quite another thing to say that an All-Good God and an All-Powerful God placed such tremendous burdens upon Helen Keller in order by those means to test her and build up her character.

But why test? And what of the people who ought to be tested but aren't? What of those who do not seem to be tested at all? If God is Omniscient He knows about the outcome of Helen Keller's struggle. Why build up character in this way? What of the characters that were destroyed? Suffering may bring man nearer to God and show man how insignificant, insufficient, dependent, and lowly he is in comparison to God. But why would a Just God, an All-Loving God, and an Omnipotent God want to create such a subservient creature? And why would He employ such drastic means?

Good does sometimes come out of evil. An epidemic produces cooperation among men, new medical techniques for treating a disease, and cures for other diseases. Wars can produce new homes, roads, better automated industries, and many jobs. But there are other ways of looking at this. Evil comes out of evil and sometimes evil comes out of good. Hardly any evil occurs that is not, or cannot be seen to be, beneficial in some way or to someone. Hardly any good occurs when there is not some reverberation or repercussion that cannot be called bad or evil. In none of these possibilities though are we able to conclude that there is Someone manipulating things to express these combinations of evil/good. Good and evil may be our reactions to the multifarious patterns found in existence, but not to the means employed by a Supreme Power.

8.8   Evil Is Necessary in Order to Arrive at a Good—or at the Ultimate Good. Evil *must* exist because without it the good cannot be be achieved. One has an infected wisdom tooth. The good is to be rid of the pain and have healthy gums and general good health. One has to go through a lot of evil such as injections, drilling, pain, surgery, all of which one accepts and allows so that one's goal of health can be attained. So with God. He must allow the existence of evil because this is His means of arriving at a good.

> It is true that people have to suffer pain in order to recover health, our medical knowledge being what it is, and the laws of nature (particularly of biology in this case) being what they are. But this consideration, which does justify a physician in inflicting pain on a patient in order that the patient may recover, applies only to limited beings who can achieve the end *in no other way.* Once we suspect, however, that the physician could achieve the goal *without* inflicting suffering on his patient, and that he is inflicting it anyway, we call him a cruel and sadistic monster. Now God, unlike the physician, is omnipotent; he could bring about a recovery without making the patient go through the excruciating pain. Why then does he not do this? If it is objected that this would require a miracle and that it would upset the orderliness of nature to continually perform miracles, it can be replied that the laws of nature could have been so set up that no miracle would be required in each case. After all, who is the author of the laws of nature? Why did God set up the causal order in such a way as to require his creatures to die in pain and agony? There is not the excuse in the case of God that there is in the case of the surgeon who can bring about his patient's recovery *only* by causing suffering; for God, being omnipotent as well as benevolent, could easily bring about the recovery without such means; indeed, he could have kept the patient from being sick in the first place. What would we think of a surgeon who first infected his child's leg and then decided to amputate it, although a cure was within his power to give and the infection was of his own giving to begin with? But this would be precisely the position of an omnipotent God. A physician who is benevolent but not omnipotent can be excused for causing suffering only because the end can be achieved in no other way; but this is precisely what is not the case with the omnipotent God, for, being omnipotent, he does not need to use evil means to bring about a good end.[4]

A person might accept his own pain and the pain in the world as part of a necessary means to an Ultimate Good. This is one of the possible ways of adjusting to pain and suffering. But some amount of sheer blind

4. John Hospers, *An Introduction to Philosophical Analysis,* 2d ed. © 1967, pp. 463–64. Reprinted by permission of Prentice-Hall, Inc., Englewood Cliffs, New Jersey.

faith and/or self-deception is necessary in anyone who emphatically declares to know what that Ultimate Good is toward which God is aiming with the use of evil as His means.

8.9 The Universe Seen as a Whole Is Good; Only the Parts Are Evil.

There are some paintings which when seen close up are ugly. Seen from a distance as a whole the parts which appeared ugly fit together in a pattern, each necessarily contributing in its own way to the beauty of the painting as a whole. So with the Universe. When immersed in it we call its parts evil, ugly, discordant, haphazard. But if we were to see the Universe as a Whole, we would find all these seemingly evil parts fitting together into a general Good.

This argument assumes what it must prove. Supposing we did have an objective, distant view of the Universe. What guarantee do we have that it would not be ugly or totally evil from that vantage point? Perhaps the Universe would be neither good nor beautiful. Perhaps such categories are not applicable to the Universe as a Whole. Perhaps the Universe isn't a Whole to be seen or conceived in that way. Perhaps what we regard as good seen close up might be seen to be evil when observed from a distance, contributing to the ugliness of the Whole.

Whether or not that evil a man sees close up is truly evil, his mistaken interpretation of it is unnecessary if God is Omnipotent and Omnibenevolent. In so far as evil in the parts exists, evil to that extent exists and is made no less evil merely because it fits into a larger Whole. The napalm burns on a child's body are evil. That may be enough to convince us that regardless of its contribution to the Good of the Whole it is still ugly, evil, and unnecessary in the light of Omnipotence and Omnibenevolence.

8.10 The Good Would Not Be Known and Appreciated Unless Evil Existed.

To know means to be able to make contrasts. To know beauty, one must know ugliness. To know darkness one must know light. To know hot one must know cold. But does evil have to occur in order for us to know what good is? Could we still know the good with less evil in existence? Do I know what murder means only when murders are committed? I can recognize and know and appreciate many things without their contrast existing in reality. This can be done by the use of definitions and imagination.

The actual existence of evil is not a condition for my knowing good. It is not a matter that to have good I must have evil existing. It is essential that for me to know what the good is I must be able to contrast it with an idea of evil. This is the minimal requirement. The same would apply to evil. It is true that I cannot forgive someone without there being some wrong or injury to be forgiven. To forgive implies the existence of something to forgive. But I can know its meaning without there being any wrong or injury in the world. Is it worthwhile having injuries or wrongs existing in reality so that the actual act of forgiveness can occur?

8.11 God and the Existence of Natural Evil. There are at least two general problems of evil. One has to do with natural evil and the other with moral evil. We have lumped them together under one heading. Moral evil refers to actions which men do which are wrong and for which we hold them morally responsible because they could have, and should have, done otherwise. Examples would be the infliction of unnecessary pain upon others, cheating, committing a crime, warring, using people as objects for purely selfish reasons. Natural evil refers to events such as famine, floods, disease, earthquakes, hurricanes, and pestilence over which man has little control but which cause him undue hardships and suffering. Moral evil and natural evil are intimately related to each other on many occasions.

Famine may be due to a natural calamity, but it also may be related to the greed of those who are in control of the food stockpiles. Then there are occasions where there are many natural evils which could have been avoided had men used forethought and coordinated their activities. Oftentimes natural evil and moral evil cannot be clearly distinguished as in the unintentional consequences of a man's action. This can take various forms: ignorance, omission, uncontrollability, or accidents of timing. Still the problem is to make both moral and natural evils compatible with God's Benevolence and Omnipotence. The Problem of Evil in the context of natural evil is how to explain the existence of such things as natural disasters. Can't an All-Good and an Omnipotent God prevent or at least lessen natural evils? How are we to show that rabies from a dog's bite, or encephalitis contracted from a canary, are compatible with God's Goodness and Power? So far we have seen a trend of thought stressing that these natural evils are a necessary and inevitable ingredient in God's Good Purposes. God cannot avoid doing things this way. Natural evils must exist in the world. This kind of answer would suffice even if we did not have a God-concept to contend with. One could then argue: it is impossible for there not to be natural evils in the world as long as man is as he is and has the ability to judge between good and evil. It is possible for there to be more or less evil in the world but not possible that there be no natural evil. The existence of natural evil would be an indubitable fact—though its amount could vary. It is an impossibility for natural evil not to exist.

The task of the God-concept approach to the existence of evil is to show that God's Power can overcome natural evil (or any kind of evil), if God wanted to use His power for this purpose. This is not asking God's Omnipotence to do the logically impossible. It is logically possible for an Omnipotent God to have created a lawful Universe without any natural evil in it. God presumably decided upon the laws of the Universe. There is no contradiction in saying that these laws could have been created in such a way that they would not produce rabies or encephalitis or syphillis. We are not asking God to create a contradiction or do the logically impossible. We are asking why God doesn't use His Omnipotence to eliminate, or at least lessen, natural evils if He is All-Good.

It has often been said that natural evils exist to test man, or to warn man of God's Power, or to punish man for the evils he has caused. This is intensely anthropomorphic as if natural evils were intentionally put there by a Being for these purposes. There are more rational ways of testing, warning, and punishing. It is also somewhat disturbing to argue that God is Good in using natural evils to punish men for all the moral evils they commit upon each other. Punishment of this sort is applied indiscriminately. The innocent are punished with the guilty. Some guilty do not even get punished at all. Why punish in that random way? Why train or educate in that inefficient manner? Punishment and testing and warning of this sort should be meted out in a better way so that it can rehabilitate man, correct him, and inspire him with dedication and motivation to follow the right path.

It has often been said that the innocent who suffer from natural and moral Evils will in the end be recompensed in the life hereafter. That does not lessen the suffering and injustices experienced in this life. It is also to presuppose that there is an afterlife, and that there will be a rational distribution of justice at some time by an Omnibenevolent God. What if it is unjust in the first place to have allowed such undeserved suffering and preventable agonies among the innocents? We would not feel it just to allow a powerful dictator sadistically to manipulate our loved ones on the ground that he will in due time give recompense with money, land, fame, influence, and power. Why are our feelings different with God? Would not an Omnipotent, Omnibenevolent God be interested in the here and now and prevent natural and moral evil from befalling those who have not deserved it?

8.12 *Evil Is Caused by Our Free Will.* How can moral evil, which we defined in the previous section as being caused by man, be reconciled with God's Omnipotence, Omnibenevolence, and Omniscience? God created man with free will, the ability to choose between good and evil. (This involves the further assumption that God has put evil in the world to choose from. Why would an Omnibenevolent God do this? And if He were Omniscient what would be the purpose of it?) Sometimes man freely chooses to do evil and that is why we have evil. God does not create evil but man's sinful nature brings it about. Man, not God, is responsible for the existence of moral evil. Since Adam and Eve, man has been in a state of original sin. Most of what he does is conditioned by a flaw in his being. He may want to do good when he knows and sees it but he is impelled by internal drives which he cannot resist to do evil. God's only other and less attractive choice was to make man a puppet without free will.

Why did an Omnipotent, Omnibenevolent God create man with a fatal flaw toward an irrestible evil? If God is Omnipotent, He then can create a Universe without moral evil, or with less of it to choose from. If God is Omnipotent, He then can create a Universe without that kind of free will, or with less of the kind which leads to destruction and cruelty and suffering. These things are logically possible. There is a wide range of choices among good, creative things from which man can freely choose. These do not involve violence, deceit, killing, assaults, inhumanity. There can be innumerable acts of free choice without causing the amount of moral evil that now exists. There are many things about which man is not free such as jumping to the moon, eating anything around him, not having to eat at all, or not breathing. We do not object to these limitations on our freedom. Why not accept a few other limitations from a Benevolent God which then would prevent us from moral evil? Man is free to commit the most heinous crimes. Because of the free will of men, millions of innocent people die in wars or in gas chambers.

Why does an Omnipotent, Benevolent God allow this kind of free will? Is it worth giving to man if these are the consequences? Could not God have given man a more limited degree of free will so that he would not and could not perform the atrocities he does? God created man with the limitations he has. Why couldn't He have created man with limitations on his evil, sinful tendencies? Just because man would not be free to harm others or to create so much moral evil does not mean that man becomes an automaton. There are instances where God favors a man with His Grace whereby that man automatically chooses to do God's Will. That man is not called a puppet or automaton. He is glorified by man and loved by God. An Omnipotent God can create man with greater strength and direction of will to resist moral evil. Being Omnibenevolent why doesn't He do it? Can we excuse such inaction?

The problem is worsened when we consider Omniscience. The argument might claim that man is capable of initiating actions entirely free from any antecedent causal conditions and thus God is absolved of responsibility since He is not the cause. But this would be wrong. Nothing can happen against the Will of God if He is Omnipotent and Omniscient. God is the Sustaining Cause of everything in the Universe. An Omnipotent and Omniscient God is at least the indirect cause of man's wrong choices as well as his free will. Such a God would be able to prevent the moral evil of man that he sees going to happen. If God doesn't do this then He must share the blame for the existence of such evil as well as for the existence of the evildoer.

If man could act against God's Will, or if man could do an act not willed by God, then we would have to admit that God is not Omnipotent, because not everything He wills to happen happens. If something happened which God did not know about then God would not be Omniscient. For God to know everything that does and will happen requires that His Power be exercised to that effect. All things come about without exception as God sees them. This Omniscience would not be possible without God's Omnipotent Control to bring things about in the manner in which they are known to occur. God has pre-determined the Universe and man's part in it. If God has so pre-determined the Universe then man cannot really be free. (Freedom would be, if anything at all, an illusion.) If man is not free then the argument that evil is due to man's free will evaporates. God, not man, would be responsible for all evil. He had the Power and Goodness to predetermine a completely different Universe.

Bibliography

Introduction to Philosophy Textbooks

Beardsley, Monroe C., and Beardsley, Elizabeth Lane. *Philosophical Thinking: An Introduction.* New York: Harcourt, Brace and World, 1965.

Danto, Arthur. *What Philosophy Is. A Guide to the Elements.* New York: Harper & Row, 1968. Paperback.

Hospers, John. *An Introduction to Philosophical Analysis.* Englewood Cliffs, N.J.: Prentice-Hall, 1967.

Nielsen, Kai. *Reason and Practice.* New York: Harper and Row, 1971.

Olson, Robert. *A Short Introduction to Philosophy.* New York: Harcourt, Brace and World, 1967. Paperback.

Randall, John H., Jr., and Buchler, Justus. *Philosophy: An Introduction.* New York: Barnes & Noble, 1942. Paperback.

Scriven, Michael. *Primary Philosophy.* New York: McGraw-Hill, 1966.

Sprague, Elmer. *What is Philosophy? A Short Introduction.* New York: Oxford University Press, 1961. Paperback.

Stroll, Avrum, and Popkin, Richard H. *Philosophy and the Human Spirit: A Brief Introduction.* New York: Holt, Rinehart and Winston, 1973. Paperback.

Williams, George. *Man Asks Why: A Programmed Sourcebook of Philosophy for Beginners.* Columbus, Ohio: Charles E. Merrill, 1973.

Philosophy Anthologies

Bronstein, Daniel J.; Krikorian, Yervant H.; and Wiener, Philip P., eds. *Basic Problems of Philosophy.* Englewood Cliffs, N. J.: Prentice-Hall, 1964.

Burr, John R., and Goldinger, Milton, eds. *Philosophy and Contemporary Issues.* New York: Macmillan, 1972.

Edwards, Paul, and Pap, Arthur, eds. *A Modern Introduction to Philosophy. Readings from Classical and Contemporary Sources.* New York: The Free Press, 1973.

Gould, James A., ed. *Classic Philosophical Questions.* Columbus, Ohio: Charles E. Merrill, 1971. Paperback.

Hospers, John, ed. *Readings in Introductory Philosophical Analysis.* Englewood Cliffs, N. J.: Prentice-Hall, 1968. Paperback.

Margolis, Joseph, ed. *An Introduction to Philosophical Inquiry. Contemporary and Classic Sources.* New York: Random House, 1970.

Sprague, Elmer, and Taylor, Paul W., eds. *Knowledge and Value.* New York: Harcourt, Brace & World, 1967.

Stein, George P., ed. *The Forum of Philosophy: An Introduction to Problem and Process.* New York: McGraw-Hill, 1973. Paperback.

Struhl, Paula Rothenberg, and Struhl, Karsten, eds. *Philosophy Now, An Introductory Reader.* New York: Random House, 1972.

Stumpf, Samuel Enoch. *Philosophical Problems. Selected Readings.* New York: McGraw-Hill, 1971. Paperback.

Philosophy of Religion Textbooks

Ducasse, C. J. *The Philosophical Scrutiny of Religion.* New York: Ronald Press, 1953.

Flew, Antony. *God and Philosophy.* London: Hutchinson & Co., 1966.

Hick, John. *Philosophy of Religion.* Englewood Cliffs, N. J.: Prentice-Hall, 1963. Paperback.

Kaufmann, Walter. *Critique of Religion and Philosophy.* Garden City, N. Y.: Anchor Books, Doubleday, 1967. Paperback.

Martin, C. B., *Religious Belief.* Ithaca, N. Y.: Cornell University Press, 1967.

Matson, Wallace I. *The Existence of God.* Ithaca, N. Y.: Cornell University Press, 1965. Paperback.

McPherson, Thomas. *The Philosophy of Religion.* New York: D. Van Nostrand, 1965. Paperback.

Munitz, Milton. *The Mystery of Existence.* New York: Appleton-Century-Crofts, 1965.

Stace, Walter T. *Religion and the Modern Mind.* New York: J. B. Lippincott, 1960. Paperback.

Philosophy of Religion Anthologies

Abernathy, George L., and Langford, Thomas A., eds. *Philosophy of Religion. A Book of Readings.* New York: Macmillan, 1962.

Alston, William, ed. *Religious Belief and Philosophical Thought. Readings in The Philosophy of Religion.* Burlingame, N. Y.: Harcourt, Brace and World, 1963.

Bronstein, Daniel J., and Schulweis, Harold M., eds. *Approaches To The Philosophy Of Religion.* Englewood Cliffs, N. J.: Prentice-Hall, 1955.

Burrill, Donald R., ed. *The Cosmological Arguments.* Garden City, N. Y.: Anchor Books, Doubleday, 1967. Paperback.

Hick, John, ed. *Classical and Contemporary Readings in the Philosophy of Religion.* Englewood Cliffs, N. J.: Prentice-Hall, 1964.

————. *The Existence of God.* New York: Macmillan, 1964. Paperback. Problems of Philosophy series, Paul Edwards, General Editor.

Hick, John, and McGill, Arthur C., eds. *The Many-faced Argument. Recent studies on the Ontological Argument for the Existence of God.* New York: Macmillan, 1967. Paperback.

Hook, S., ed. *Religious Experience and Truth.* London: Oliver and Boyd Ltd., 1962.

Pike, Nelson, ed. *God and Evil.* Englewood Cliffs, N. J.: Prentice-Hall, 1964. Paperback.

Plantinga, Alvin, ed. *The Ontological Argument from St. Anselm to Contemporary Philosophers.* Garden City, N. Y.: Anchor Books, Doubleday, 1965. Paperback.

Rowe, William, and Wainwright, William J., eds. *Philosophy of Religion: Selected Readings.* New York: Harcourt Brace and Jovanovich, 1973.

Weinberg, Julius R., and Yandell, Keith A., eds. *Philosophy of Religion.* New York: Holt, Rinehart and Winston, 1971. Paperback.

Comparative Religions Textbooks

Archer, John Clark. *Faiths Men Live By.* New York: Thomas Nelson, 1934.

Bahm, Archie J. *The World's Living Religions.* New York: Dell, 1964. Paperback.

Lyon, Quinter Marcellus. *The Great Religions.* New York: Odyssey Press, 1957.

Noss, John B. *Man's Religions.* New York: Macmillan, 1956.

Smith, Huston. *The Religions of Man.* New York: Harper Colophon Books, 1964.

Wheelwright, Philip. *The Burning Fountain.* Bloomington: Indiana University Press, 1954.

Index